·THE HANDMADE·
TEARDROP TRAILER

DESIGN & BUILD A CLASSIC TINY CAMPER FROM SCRATCH

The opinions expressed in this book are the author's own and do not
necessarily reflect the views of Spring House Press.

Publisher: Paul McGahren
Editorial Director: Matthew Teague
Editor: Kerri Grzybicki
Design: Lindsay Hess
Layout: Jodie Delohery
Photography and Illustrations: Matt Berger, unless otherwise indicated
Cover Photographer: Lincoln Else

Photography credits: Alchemy Coffee (16 upper right, 20); Madeline Berger
(106–108); Mary Hadley Berger (45 far left); Nina Berger (202); Tom Brickman
(21); Lincoln Else (cover and 36–37); Mark Janke (16 lower right, 24–26); Justin
Kuechle and Jessica Miano (16, bottom left, 22–23); Glenn Ross (16 upper left,
17–19); Overland Trailer customers (27); Windy Nation (141).

Spring House Press
P.O. Box 239
Whites Creek, TN 37189

ISBN: 978-1-940611-65-5

Library of Congress Control Number: 2018959984

Printed in The United States of America

10 9 8 7 6 5 4 3 2 1

Note: The following list contains names used in *The Handmade Teardrop
Trailer* that may be registered with the United States Copyright Office: 3M
(Marine Adhesive Sealant Fast Cure 5200); Alchemy Coffee; Amazon; Apple
(Apple Pencil, iPad); Bluetooth; Container Store; Entropy Resins (Super Sap
CLR); Filon; Forest River, Inc.; Google; Grain Surfboards; Honda (Odyssey);
IKEA; National Association of Trailer Manufacturers; Overland Trailer; Paper
by 53; Ryobi; Popular Homecraft, Popular Mechanics; Society of Automotive
Engineers; SPAX; Stanley (Surform); Tabet Manufacturing Company, Inc.
(Hurricane Hinge); Tetris; Titebond2; Vintage Technologies; West System;
WindyNation; YouTube.

The information in this book is given in good faith; however, no warranty is
given, nor are results guaranteed. Woodworking is inherently dangerous.
Your safety is your responsibility. Neither Spring House Press nor the authors
assume any responsibility for any injuries or accidents.

To learn more about Spring House Press books, or to find a retailer near you,
email info@springhousepress.com or visit us at www.springhousepress.com.

·THE HANDMADE·

TEARDROP TRAILER

DESIGN & BUILD A CLASSIC TINY CAMPER FROM SCRATCH

Matt Berger

SPRING HOUSE PRESS

CONTENTS

"The Painted Desert"

Introduction:
A TRAILER LIFE

It's an unexpected place to begin, but I will: It all started back in the '80s, in the bathroom of my family home in San Francisco's East Bay, sitting on the toilet way longer than required, lost in the pages of *Trailer Life* magazine.

Looking back, this could be the moment I first embodied my true identity as an old man trapped in the body of a boy—studying trailer floor plans and technical specifications while my friends shot hoops.

I know exactly what it was that kept me glued to the glossy RV magazine pages: All the comforts of home, efficiently laid out in a structurally sound house on wheels, combined with the feeling you get on a camping trip with family and friends, prepared for anything.

The centerfold spreads in each issue showed glorious panoramas of 20-some-foot trailers perched on a bluff, overlooking a shiny lake or rugged coastline. A striped sun shade, extending over a fold-out dining table as Mom emerged from the tiny kitchen like a magician with a tray of sizzling bacon, scrambled eggs, and warm buttery biscuits.

Photographs of the interior showed off a spacious master bedroom for parents and two bunkbeds for the kids; a bathroom with a shower; and a small kitchen not missing a thing. The living room was just an arm's reach away, with a couch-by-day folded out to a double bed for guests at night. Behind, above, and underneath all of that was storage for board games, flashlights, sleeping bags, and swim gear. And how could I leave out the TV and VCR? This is 1980, people. A TV and VCR!

The reason our bathroom was stocked with *Trailer Life* had to do with my new extended family. My mom remarried, resulting in the merging of two families and me becoming the youngest of eight.

With my new family came a 26-foot Wilderness trailer, towed behind the bumper of a 1980 Ford F150, that took us each summer to places etched as memories in my mind: the painted desert of Arizona; the high mesas of New Mexico; the agate beaches of the Oregon coast; the edge of Northern California's Feather River; lakeside in a summer trailer community filled with families like mine, where each day a gargantuan potluck dinner emerged atop a banquet-sized picnic table, friends dishing and laughing,

kids playing into the night until the last flashlight turned dark.

HISTORY OF THE TEARDROP TRAILER

My family was part of a tradition of hitting the road with an automobile and a half-ton homestead on wheels that started around the turn of the 20th century.

In 1908, Ford Motor Co. introduced its transformative automobile, the Model T. To accommodate America's new love of the open road, our great-grandparents spent centuries dutifully grading and paving roads that reached far and wide to connect the most unexpected places.

"I believe the first teardrop trailer was built in someone's barn," says Mark Janke, a teardrop trailer historian and co-owner of Overland Trailer Co. in the Pacific Northwest. "It may have been the next natural evolution in the wagon or, more likely, was designed to be pulled by the early automobiles like the model T." As Mark explains it, those early cars didn't have a lot of pulling capacity, so whatever people made needed to be light and small. As it turns out, in October 1918 a gentleman named Francis W. Houser of Gering, Nebraska, filed a patent for his tiny camper "Trailer," and earned a patent for it a year later.

"The object of this invention is to provide means whereby motor-car tourists and campers may readily transport from place to place articles of bedding, dishes or other necessities without consuming space in the motor vehicle and thereby subjecting the occupants of the vehicle to inconvenience and discomfort."

INTRODUCTION: A TRAILER LIFE

About 1,500 hundred miles away in Dubois, Pennsylvania, inventor Ninian R. Moore filed a patent in March 1919 for a similar object of invention "to provide a compact dust and weather proof container for sleeping and cooking equipment in the form of an automobile trailer which maybe quickly transformed into complete sleeping and cooking compartments and quickly returned to traveling condition."

By the late 1930s, Congress called for the creation of a free Interstate system that would connect the nation by road.

With the road about to be literally paved, the 1940s brought an explosion in new trailer designs to market, just as another national movement was taking place in garage shops across the country. Back then, people used their garages to build, fix, and tinker. The American suburban garage was abuzz with activity: soap box derby carts, scooters, the earliest incarnations of the handmade skateboard, tree houses, and backyard forts.

Over the next two decades, more patents and innovations took root. Soon, these garage-shop inventions

"Lost Hills, California"

"Bixby Bridge, Big Sur"

were showing up in popular how-to magazines. The March/April 1939 issue of *Popular Homecraft* ran a story and plans for a teardrop trailer designed and built by Louis Rogers of Pasadena, California. A year later, *Popular Mechanics* came out with its own version of the diminutive pull-behind house on wheels. The February 1940 edition introduced one of the most iconic DIY tiny trailer designs to date. The so-called "Midget Trailer" to "serve your vacation needs" measured slightly more than 6 feet tall, 5 feet wide, and 12 feet from hitch to bumper.

World War II put a pause in the DIY trailer trend, but after WWII, the mobile home industry was re-invigorated. Suddenly there were surpluses of steel and aluminum. Teardrop companies sprang up everywhere. The trailers were affordable and easily towed.

Starting in 1945, C.W. "Bill" Worman and Andy Anderson produced Kit Kamper teardrop trailers. At its peak, Kit was turning out as many as 40 trailers a day. A total of 4,500 Kit Kampers were produced in 1946 and 1947. During that same time, a pair of southern California entrepreneurs started the Kenskill Company and made about 200 teardrop trailers by hand during the summers of 1946 and 1947. In September of 1947, Howard Warren of Riverside, California, published his do-it-yourself plans for a teardrop in *Mechanix Illustrated.* A flurry of patents for collapsible and convertible camper trailers followed.

"Down by the River"

The 1960s and 1970s brought new innovations to the RV industry. Road safety laws were enacted, and trailer makers were forced to improve their products. Simple wood frames evolved into welded metal-frame construction. Crash testing led to innovations. The introduction of vehicles with a V8 engine meant the teardrop's popularity started to wane, as trailers got bigger and grander. 1978 was a boom year for RVs—389,000 sold.

Just one year later, that boom was met with a big bust. A gas crisis left RV owners holding the keys to major guzzlers. Most of the major manufacturers went out of business or at least pulled back production. In 1980, new orders plummeted nearly 75 percent.

It took a few years, but the industry started to rebound in the mid-1980s. The return of cheap gas meant more people were hitting roads in cars and campers. Trailer manufacturers were also taking their designs to the next level. Bigger was better, and electronics and compact mechanical parts introduced new luxuries to the campground experience, such as pop-out walls that provided an extra living room, or whole-trailer entertainment systems with satellite television that brought the comforts of home to the most remote campsite.

The popularity of the camper trailer over the past decade continues to match trends with gas prices at the pump. The connection was seen again in 2009; during the depths of the Great Recession, trailer sales plummeted.

In the second decade of the 21st century, as the economy recovers and more vacationers stayed closer to home, the market for RVs rebounded once again. Today as many as 9 million RVs are on the roads in the United States. It's estimated that 22 million people took an RV trip in the summer of 2017.

As I get older and raise my own family, I think a lot about giving my kids lasting memories of their own. That inspired the year-long journey captured in this book of building a teardrop trailer from scratch in my garage. Like the quintessential family road trip, this project was full of adventure, pitfalls, and triumphs, and provided me with a lifetime of memories to tow around with me.

"Alpine Campfire"

1

DESIGN YOUR OWN

Building your own tiny trailer from scratch starts with inspiration, but it takes grit and a good design to succeed. Also keep in mind that when you commit to a DIY project as large as a teardrop trailer, you're also making a commitment to neighbors and strangers with whom you share parking spots and public roads. I won't beat around the bush: let's make it our pledge not to build a cut-rate trailer that makes the rest of the world suffer in its presence.

Visual and aesthetic design are important. Your trailer should be something that you're proud to tow. But that's just for looks.

A focus on structural integrity and drivability is also a top concern. Your trailer should tow safely on public roads in all weather and driving conditions.

There's also the issue of health and safety. A trailer that leaks water can quickly grow mold or mildew and become uninhabitable. Preventing water intrusion and managing the water that does sneak through the cracks should be a top concern with every design decision you make.

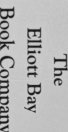

Inspiration everywhere

Like many of you, I began my trailer with little knowledge about the task at hand. I had experience with woodworking tools, designing furniture, and building projects around the house but had never taken on a project of this complexity.

I began with my usual approach—find smart people, ask a lot of questions, and learn from their mistakes and successes.

I started with late-night web surfing. Soon I was itching to see the real thing up close. You know that feeling when you are shopping for something big—like a new car—and suddenly you see the make and model you want everywhere you look? That's true when it comes to trailers, too.

I was surrounded by them, so why not study them? I started pulling over to inspect random trailers. I crouched down to see how the body attached to the frame. I stood on tippy toes to see how the roof joined to the walls, or how the doors sealed shut. I inspected the materials used (and not used). Where was the center of gravity? How was the weight distributed front to back and side to side? Where were the wheels and axle located?

The conclusion I came to is every trailer is similar, but requires a unique approach to materials and construction based on its function and purpose.

The goal of this chapter is to help you explore your design and material options, and understand the consequences of each decision you make. Now is the time to set yourself up for success.

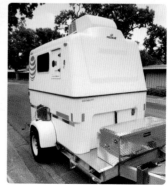

Sage advice from the teardrop trailer community

There are thousands of teardrop trailers on the road; the majority are made one at a time, by hand, in someone's garage. DIY builders have been doing this for decades with great success (and many failures). If there's anything I've learned in life, it's to pay attention to both. After getting started, I decided to track down a handful of builders who, like me, started with an idea and some inspiration and ended up as the proud owner of a tiny trailer. Though I didn't take all of the advice, it is here for your benefit. Note: images are provided by each owner.

The Artist: Glenn Ross designed his one-of-a-kind teardrop with a unique, waterproof exterior.

The Alchemist: Owner Evan Spivak hired builder Tom Brickman to create his teardrop coffee shop.

Family Heirloom: Justin and Jess built a trailer for their growing family.

The Historians: The owners of Overland Trailer turned their hobby into a burgeoning business.

The Artist
Canvas Caravanner, Glenn Ross

The first teardrop trailer that caught my attention and inspired me to think differently about design and construction beyond the classic teardrop was built by Glenn Ross of Coquitlam, British Columbia, Canada.

Matt Berger: *What was the most challenging aspect of your build?*

Glenn Ross: One of my main challenges was to build a hatch that would never leak. Teardrop trailers, both DIY and professionally built, are plagued with leaky hatches: type "teardrop leaky hatch" into Google and you will see. Once inside a structure, water seems to defy gravity and physics, and will infiltrate deep into the trailer structure and ruin it.

I set out to design a set of mechanical details that would be watertight without the use of rubber seals or silicone. I broke the design down into four distinct challenges: the membrane, water redirection, the gutter, and a failsafe.

MB: *Your trailer has a unique exterior. Can you tell me about it?*

GR: The merit of using a canvas and paint membrane is that it creates one continuous membrane, with no seams, across the entire external structure, including the hatch details and gutter.

There are other ways to do this, so experiment a little if you are considering using it. I used painter's drop cloths. They are totally adequate—although next time I will source something a little more refined. Wash and iron your canvas. It shrinks, and the wrinkles will not disappear when you apply it.

A canvas maché—canvas and glue—skin provides a smooth, waterproof finish for the trailer exterior.

MB: *How does the canvas get applied?*
GR: I use Titebond 2 adhesive. I went to a wholesaler and bought a 5-gallon pail. Mayonnaise squeeze bottles make great glue bottles. Foam rollers are the main tool to spread the glue, although sometimes you will need a brush. Don't rinse them out every time you use them; wrap them in plastic. Be generous with the glue, and plan to do one section at a time.

Do the tricky bits first, then the big pieces. This was my basic approach, although there are times when it is better to do the details after. Canvas can be stretched, compressed, and manipulated quite a bit. I tested the limits on scrap wood before doing some of the details.

I found it easiest to clean up the edges after applying the canvas. Use a sharp knife. It works best when the glue is nearly set but not totally dry. You can sand the glue residue off before applying the last layer of canvas—everything will show through.

When you get to the main parts, take your time and keep everything clean. I use a wood block to smooth and flatten the canvas once it is on the plywood. You have quite a bit of time to get it perfect. It will look pretty bad until you get the paint on. The important thing at this point is not how it looks, but that it is smooth.

MB: *So once the skin is on, what's next?*
GR: Buy the best latex outdoor paint you can. I used porch and deck paint. The fabric absorbs a lot of paint—I used 4 gallons. Really saturate the fabric on the first layer. When it dries, it still won't look very good. You can sand between coats to remove the little fabric nubs, and generally smooth each layer. By the time you get to the fourth coat of paint, it should look smooth and shiny (or satin in my case).

MB: *You talk a lot about managing water in addition to keeping it out. Can you expand on that?*
GR: My primary line of defense is to direct the water run-off away from the hatch openings. A ridge on the roof directs water away from the hatch, and off the side of the trailer. The hatch itself also has a ridge on its sides to direct water down and out of the seam.

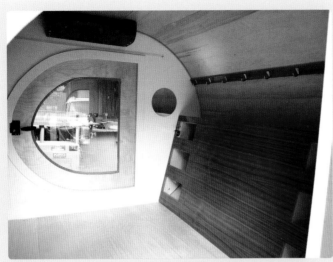

The interior features vacuum laminated parts covered with decorative veneer.

The painted canvas membrane creates a continuous waterproof surface across the entire exterior of the trailer.

The gutter takes care of the water that makes its way into the seam of the hatch door. It is important to include a drip edge on the hatch itself, so that water does not migrate across the inside surface of the hatch. The gutter system also must work when the hatch is open. A drip edge is critical.

The interior of the hatch is waterproofed with the same paint and canvas membrane as the exterior. If water does make it into the hatch, it will still not be able to infiltrate the interior of the trailer, or the structure of the walls.

MB: *What would you change if you did this again?*
GR: I'm already making my next trailer, and the big change is that I'm going to

The Alchemist
A Teardrop Coffee Shop

The story of this unique teardrop trailer comes from builder Tom Brickman, who sent me this uplifting story of how Richmond, Virginia got its first teardrop coffee shop. Tom writes:

Eric Spivack of Alchemy Coffee approached me to design a trailer that would house him and an entire coffee shop's worth of equipment on a 4 x 8-foot platform. Having worked in, designed, and built more than 30 restaurants, I said "OK." It seemed an impossible feat, which excited me.

After an ergonomic working flow, equipment list, and electric and plumbing needs were discussed, it was Tetris. I had already envisioned something instantly recognizable and unique. The curved shape allowed extension from the 4 x 8-foot stock trailer bed to accommodate more storage.

After several sketches and weight distribution calculations, I choose to make the frame of welded steel tube skinned with lauan plywood to accept the redwood siding and aluminum sheet roof. The service window was custom-made, and the door was bought from an RV distributor.

Next, I attached the lauan to the frame with a special industrial adhesive and self-tapping screws. This stiffened the frame extremely! Next, we put the

On the outside: redwood siding, an aluminum roof, and a commercial RV door.

It took some careful planning to fit a food-safety-approved kitchen inside.

aluminum roof on. The frame had to be perfectly square or the sheet would not register on the frame.

With the structure built, I ran the plumbing and electric, mounted the generator, and found a gas tank to mount under the floor for wastewater storage—very happy with that solution.

I will never forget rolling it out of the shop for the first try. After many years of daily use, it has required very little maintenance. It continues to deliver great coffee and pastries to thousands of patrons. Eric was a great client, and I later designed and built his brick and mortar coffee shop.

For others going down this road: I would say always keep an open mind, try to find unconventional uses for everyday

The steel tube frame gets extra rigid when the plywood siding goes on.

Family Heirloom
Small Trailer, Big Memories

Justin Kuechle and Jessica Miano live in Eden Prairie, Minnesota with their daughter Piper and dog Luna. He's an industrial designer and she's a photographer; together they battled the cold Minnesota winter to build a teardrop trailer from scratch in their two-car garage. I asked Jessica a few questions via email and she shared this story:

Justin and I were looking at purchasing a camper in winter 2016, but we couldn't reach an agreement on what we wanted. He wanted a pop-up, and I wanted a truck camper. I decided to do a little digging and see if there was something out there we could compromise on. That was when we came across teardrops and the idea of building your own. We fell in love with all the curves and cleverness of a teardrop.

We began brainstorming what we would do to customize our camper. The more we discussed it, the more we fell in love with our imaginary camper.

Our build started in March 2017 and took place in our two-car garage in Minnesota. Due to the nature of Justin's work, we had all the tools we needed on hand and were able to find and purchase all our build materials easily from the lumberyard (plywood and ash for the trim) and online (hardware and specialty camper parts).

A stained plywood exterior and hardwood trim fit right in with woodsy Minnesota.

A large front window provides plenty of natural light by day and star-gazing by night.

The build went very smoothly, although Justin did not enjoy the process of bending pieces of plywood to fit the curves of the camper. I, on the other hand, did not appreciate the way my arms ached in protest as we stained the entire thing. But they were such small hurdles to get over and the reward on the other side was so much better than we could have hoped for.

After our build, we discussed what we could've done differently and ultimately felt that a sturdier trailer would have been worth the investment. Other than that, we felt that we had navigated the entire process quite well. We finished in June 2017, just in time for our first trip to Daly Campground in Mapleton, Minnesota. We've been all over the state now, and we

The spring-time build was ready for the campsite just in time for the Minnesota summer.

The Historians
Mark and Nathan of Overland Trailers

There are a few brave adventurers who have turned their love for DIY teardrop trailer building into more than just a hobby. That's the story of Mark Janke and Nathan Henson of Spokane, Washington. They're the two proprietors of Overland Trailer, a small-batch manufacturer of classic teardrops.

Matt Berger: *Tell me about Overland Trailer.*

Mark Janke: Our business started when I was recognized at a concert I was attending. I had built and blogged about my first home-built teardrop trailer and was starting work on a teardrop trailer documentary film (published by Amazon in 2011). At this concert, there were particularly excited teardrop fans who asked me to build them a trailer.

I called my friend and camping companion, Nathan, who had helped with the first home build. Nathan agreed to team up and Overland Trailer was born. We eventually named our trailer and new design after that family: 58 Heald.

MB: *What inspired you to go all in on teardrops?*

MJ: We love this way of camping. It is simple. It lets us just get to the adventure of camping.

The average tent camper will spend an hour a day setting up or tearing down camp as they travel. A teardrop can be

Going from building a one-off trailer to becoming a small-batch manufacturer required a different approach to the manufacturing process.

set up in under 10 minutes, and you've got a queen-sized bed, a refrigerator, and an oven. Winterization takes about 45 minutes. It is camping, but without a lot of the hassle of tenting or the complex systems of the larger RV. This ensures we can camp where we want with minimal impact on our lives or the environment, and its compact size guarantees time outside.

MB: *You know a lot about the history of teardrop trailers and provided a lot of historical details for the foreword to this book. Where did this all get started?*
MJ: Here's a question: When did Americans stop traveling in wagons, sleeping under the stars, and "roughin

of Americans leave their stationary homes in search of a temporary, more rugged, experience. This question was the genesis for our feature documentary.

MB: *Where do you physically build your trailers? Describe the space you use.*
MJ: We have a light industrial space. Originally, we made everything ourselves, but now we leverage the expertise of local business owners to water jet–cut the stainless-steel skins and CNC-rout the body sides. Everything is now accurate to parts of a millimeter. Our quality improved and our production time decreased. It was a no-brainer.

We still make all the cabinetry and weld

MB: *What are your favorite design features?*

MJ: A complete stainless-steel exterior. Yes, it is much more expensive than aluminum and a bit heavier, but we believe the benefits outweigh the costs. Stainless doesn't oxidize and turn a dull gray, is much more resistant to creasing, and is easy to clean. Overall, it adds about 45 pounds to the trailer. Our current models, dry, weigh in at 740 pounds.

We also install stainless-steel countertops in the galley. They're easy to clean up and durable for any hot pots or pans that land on them.

MB: *What advice would you give to someone interested in making one?*

MJ: Learn from others as much as you can. Get a mentor if possible. We regularly answer questions for people who may never do business with us. We're happy to help build the community. The home build is how we got started in 2007. We get it. We love it!

Really important: don't skimp on the quality of your materials. Pick quality materials that will last a long time. It sucks to build cheap and then spend the life of the trailer doing rehab on it. It also costs a lot more than if it was done right and with good materials the first time.

Don't set unattainable timelines for your build. Make sure you're making progress but doing a quality job. Once you're camping, you'll probably want to do more of that instead of putting off a camping trip to fix something that you should have done right the first time.

MB: *What are the biggest mistakes you see people like me make when we build our first trailer?*

MJ:

1. Overbuilding: The home builder who is uncertain will often build a 1,500-pound bunker on wheels. It will function fine, but the costs are more materials, more fuel, and more wear on the tow vehicle.

2. Low-grade plywood: A teardrop should be built from cabinet-grade plywood. Yes, it costs more. But it is much stronger and more stable than plywoods found at most big box stores. If there is a leak, cabinet-grade plywood also resists warping and rotting better.

A stainless-steel exterior and high-quality manufactured windows and doors ensure durability and long life.

Durable, high-quality materials can survive even the harshest environments.

Weighing in dry at around 750 pounds, it doesn't take much to tow an Overland Trailer.

3. Forgetting that it rains: It will rain, and your trailer will get very wet. If you're driving, it will be wet and there will be air pressure pushing that water into every possible little crack in your finish. Make sure your sealants are flexible and won't react with your other finishes (for instance, some silicones chemically react with aluminum); metals will also chemically react to each other and decay. Do your research. Make sure that you have no places for water when it is done but also that you haven't built in materials that will make cracks later in the life of the trailer. A good test is to hit your build with a power washer at close range. If it survives that, you're good!

4. Toilets: We've had multiple home builders write about how they installed a chemical toilet inside their trailer and it leaked and soaked into the floor. Our recommendation is always to keep the potty jobs outside.

5. Insulated walls: I made this mistake on my first trailer. It adds weight and only makes the interior a bit quieter. The thermal advantage of insulated sides is negated by the fact that campers must keep a vent or window open for fresh air.

MB: *Any final words of inspiration?*
MJ: Probably the line about the teardrop

Illustrate Your Ideas

Before I build, I draw. Use pen and paper, digital drawing tools, whatever you've got. Start sketching basic shapes and configurations whenever you have an idea that comes to mind. You can also begin to reveal complicated areas of construction and work out solutions for the ones you want to pursue or cut the ones you'll never be able to pull off. Throughout the book in each chapter you'll find additional sketches like these, some to scale, some not. The looseness of my sketches and drawings guided me through difficult construction challenges, but were flexible enough to adapt to dimensional changes on the fly. These are all drawn on iPad with Apple Pencil, using my favorite drawing app, Paper by 53. Look it up or experiment with other drawing applications until you find your favorite. And if you're more comfortable with paper and pencil, or CAD software, by all means go ahead.

Sketchbook:
AN EXPLORATION OF TRAILER DESIGN

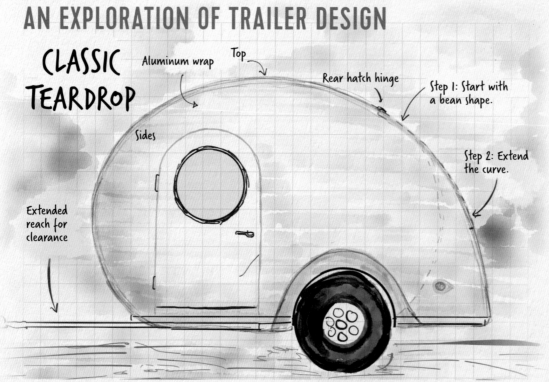

The quintessential teardrop trailer lives up to its name, with a teardrop-shaped round front that tapers to a point at the rear bumper. This all-aluminum-wrapped design, like many DIY and commercial trailers that feature a similar extended front, requires an extra-long tongue to provide adequate clearance between the vehicle and the front-end of the trailer. This concept also accommodates a tall door with almost enough clearance to stand inside.

If you want to cut down on cost and complexity when building a teardrop trailer, design it to make use of standard dimensioned lumber and sheet goods available at your local home-improvement store. Keep your side panels contained to a sheet of 4 x 8-foot plywood and you can simplify the construction to essentially just a box. Use manufactured doors, windows, and vents. Less complexity also increases your chances of succeeding with a water-tight build.

The 4 X 8 SPECIAL

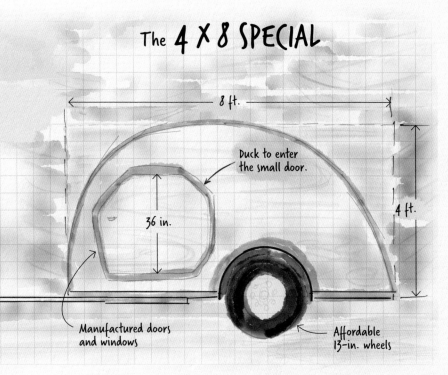

8 ft.

Duck to enter the small door.

4 ft.

36 in.

Manufactured doors and windows

Affordable 13-in. wheels

There's something about the compact side doors on teardrop trailers that bug me. No matter how well you maximize the space, they still require some level of contortion to get in and out. They definitely don't accommodate those with physical conditions. That got me thinking about a rear-hatch entryway that opened up for wide and easy access. Move the kitchen to modular compartments on each side and add a tent drop, and you've got a big open sleeping space with a panoramic view. Design your trailer to carry your bi...

REAR HATCH with a PANORAMIC VIEW

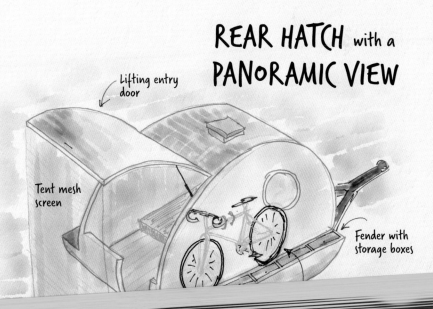

Lifting entry door

Tent mesh screen

Fender with storage boxes

Sketchbook:
AN EXPLORATION OF TRAILER DESIGN (CONTINUED)

ODE to the STUDEBAKER

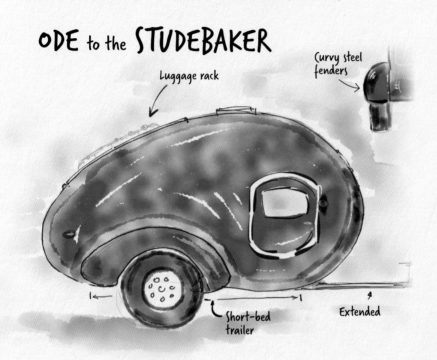

Luggage rack

Curvy steel fenders

Short-bed trailer

Extended

I took the dog on a walk recently and discovered a 1950s Studebaker parked in the neighborhood. I was impressed by the curvy lines on its front and back fenders—perfect inspiration for a teardrop. This build would require some skills in metalworking to bend the sheet metal. If you've got the skills, go for it!

The 4X4 OFF-ROADER

Luggage rack with extra structural support underneath

Side-mount storage for supplies

Durable all-metal exterior

Full-size spare

Rugged off-road tires

Jack up your trailer frame and throw on some 4x4 tires and you're on your way to the wilderness. Building an off-road trailer requires using more metal than wood. And your construction method should be able to withstand a beating from the shock of driving down a rocky road. Be sure to upgrade your tow hitch to a top-of-the line connection. And focus on extreme waterproofing during the construction process.

Sketchbook:
AN EXPLORATION OF TRAILER DESIGN (CONTINUED)

The POP-UP VENDOR

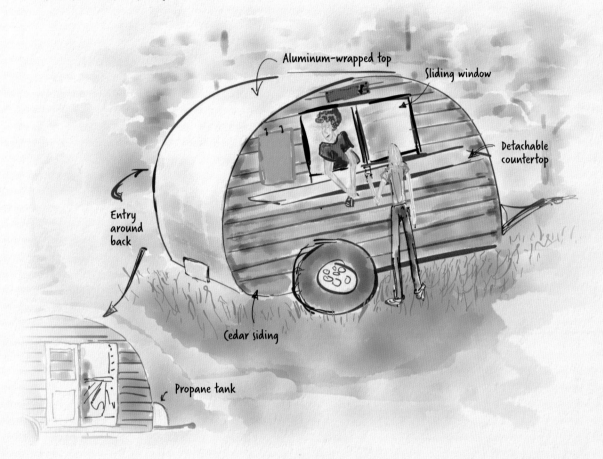

Aluminum-wrapped top

Sliding window

Detachable countertop

Entry around back

Cedar siding

Propane tank

If you run a small mobile business, forget the food truck. Build your business a tiny trailer that doubles as a street vendor booth. Store your perishable goods inside and pop-up the kitchen galley when you're ready to serve. Consider materials that are easy to wash down and disinfect to keep customers healthy and food safety inspectors happy. You'll also need to upgrade to a 110-volt AC/DC power system and generator

Sketchbook:
AN EXPLORATION OF TRAILER DESIGN (CONTINUED)

The **BOXY**

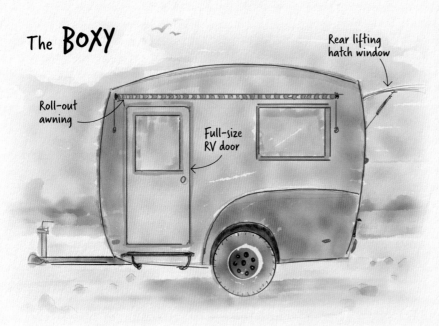

Rear lifting
hatch window

Roll-out
awning

Full-size
RV door

This little boxy design is inspired by the vintage fiberglass trailer more than a classic teardrop. There's no kitchen galley here, so you'll have to find another place to do your cooking and food prep, or relocate the kitchen inside and share space with the bed.

The **CARNY**

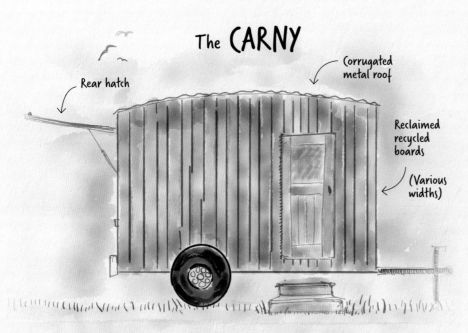

Rear hatch

Corrugated
metal roof

Reclaimed
recycled
boards

(Various
widths)

This rustic tiny trailer design would fit right in with your local traveling circus caravan. A corrugated tin roof is cheap and simple, and protects from the elements. Wood siding cobbled together from various width and species, along with a recycled door, keep the budget to a minimum and add to its bohemian look.

Sketchbook:
AN EXPLORATION OF TRAILER DESIGN (CONTINUED)

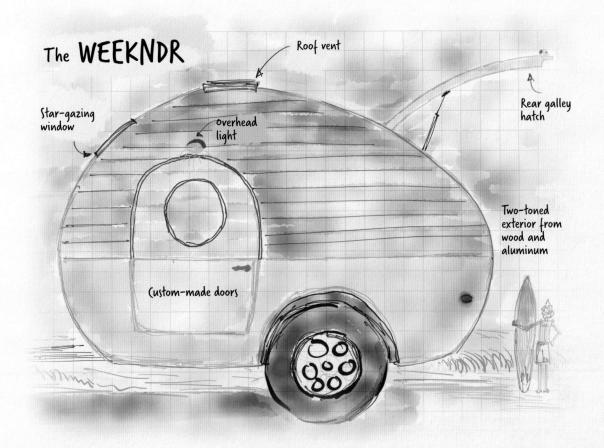

The **WEEKNDR**

Roof vent

Star-gazing window

overhead light

Rear galley hatch

Two-toned exterior from wood and aluminum

Custom-made doors

While designing the trailer for this book I kept coming back to this two-toned design—wood paneling on top and durable aluminum paneling on the bottom half to protect it against shooting rocks and debris while traveling on the road. A rear galley opens up to a simple campsite-ready kitchen and utility space. A front hatch with a screen opens to provide stargazing at night. And a roof vent cycles fresh air through the cabin, keeping you comfortable on warm summer nights.

Build a 3-D prototype

Like all garage-shop projects, my teardrop trailer started out as a pile of hand-drawn sketches. The problem with a sketch is that it doesn't consider scale and proportion. What might look good on the back of a napkin doesn't always add up in three dimensions.

Before I embark on any building project, I like to see my idea to scale in three dimensions first. My material of choice: high-density foam. Foam is easy to cut and shape. It's expendable. You can glue it, tape it, pin it, and quickly transform it into shaped parts. And just like that, your design will come to life in miniature scale.

1. Model concepts.
Use the foam model as a drawing aid to help you determine the size, dimensions and curves from all angles.

2. Nothing fancy.
Fabricating your parts is easy. Foam is simple to cut in your garage with a handsaw, or upgrade to a bandsaw for better results.

3. Build up the foam block.
Glue together pieces of foam scraps into a block to increase the size of your teardrop model.

4. Add accessories.
Create accessories like doors and windows from wood veneer and scraps.

The prototype bike trailer

Before I committed to the full-size build I decided to use that time to build a functioning prototype that I could use to test out some of my construction concepts like joinery and mechanical connections in real-world scenarios. This can often reveal flaws and rabbit holes that can lead your project down a bad path.

If you have an old kid bike trailer sitting around your garage, once it's stripped down of all its parts to a bare frame and axle, it's probably a great candidate for the base of a prototype bicycle teardrop. Though uncompleted, it tested my construction ideas and gave me the confidence to move on to the full-sized project.

1. Disassemble the trailer.
Remove everything carefully from the base, but don't undermine its structural integrity if you plan to tow it for real.

2. Make lightweight insulated panels.
Create strong, thick panels from ¼-inch plywood and rigid foam insulation.

3. Assemble the parts.

Galley hatch with Hurricane Hinge

Roof vent with 12-volt electric fan

Interior and exterior siding: Redwood panels and aluminum over plywood sheathing

Walls and framing: 2x2 framing with rigid foam insulation

Galley kitchen

Exterior 12-volt lights

Deep-cycle marine battery and on-board 12-volt electrical system

Custom trim

Travel lights and blinkers

Torsional suspension and electric brakes

Queen-sized mattress with padded headboard and storage underneath

15-in. wheels

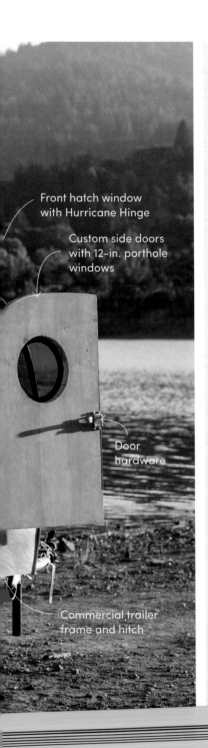

Front hatch window
with Hurricane Hinge

Custom side doors
with 12-in. porthole
windows

Door
hardware

Commercial trailer
frame and hitch

②

THE WEEKNDR

— *Caravan* —

After months of imagining, studying, drawing, and prototyping, I settled on a plan and was ready to get started. Like most projects I take on, I came up with my own construction process to best accommodate my tools, materials, skills, and shop space. A better process is possible—and you should explore the best approach for your comfort level and abilities.

For me, a key consideration was the sheer size of it all. I was building my trailer single-handedly inside an attached garage shared with the family, and a basic set of hand and power tools. None of the parts could be bigger or heavier than I could handle with my own two hands. A handful of operations did require woodworking machinery. But, for the most part, I kept things limited to a circular saw, a hand-held trim router, a chop saw, a jigsaw, and my trusty toolbox of hand tools.

I also wanted to purchase all the building materials at the local hardware store, lumber yard, and home center. A few specialty items would require mail order, but I tried to keep that to a minimum.

Features and parts

From bumper to hitch, most teardrop trailers are built from the same basic components. It's the personal touches that differentiate one trailer from another.

THE TRAILER FRAME

Just like a house needs a solid foundation, a trailer needs a trustworthy chassis and wheelbase. Don't be fooled by the promises of cheap trailers available by mail order. If it comes in a box and assembles with bolts, you probably don't want to depend on it to haul more than 1,500 pounds of steel, wood, and camping gear across the American asphalt at 60 miles per hour. Choose a trailer frame made from thick steel or aluminum, and strong welded parts. Unless you're an expert metalworker, follow my lead and purchase a trailer from a reputable dealer or custom fabricator. This will ensure you get off to a safe and sound start.

AXLE

A single axle is all that's required, and its placement is a critical factor. To achieve the perfect weight balance for towing, follow the 60-40 rule: position the axle at a midpoint where 60% of the weight is distributed in front of the axle, and 40% of the weight is distributed behind.

WHEELS

Tire size varies depending on your pocket book and your ambitions. Go big with 15-inch wheels for a smoother, softer ride. These full-sized rims and tires are the same ones you'd buy for your minivan, so they're easy to replace or repair, and they raise the trailer off the ground to the same height as your vehicle. Thanks to the trailer's light weight, you can also downgrade to the economy route with 13-inch wheels, or compromise with 14-inch wheels.

THE HITCH

For safe, comfortable towing, the trailer should attach to your vehicle with a high-quality trailer hitch and ball mount. Class III hitches come in a few sizes. I went with the recommended 2-inch ball. A bigger, heavier trailer would require a larger one. The ball mount's height from the ground is also critical to maintain the proper tongue weight, distribution, and balance when attached to your vehicle.

Start with a utility trailer that's built to your custom specifications.

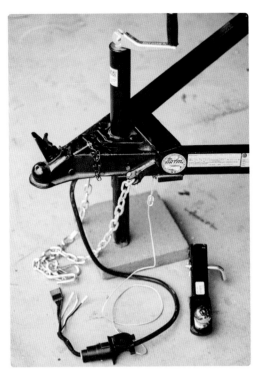

This is the standard 2-inch ball hitch and receiving coupler with all the required safety components.

Cross chains

A pair of chains welded to the trailer clip to your trailer hitch or bumper. The recommendation is to cross the chains and clip each end to the opposite side of the hitch.

Brake chain

Trailers with electric brake systems come with a built-in safety feature if you come unhitched in tow. If the trailer detaches from your car, the brake chain pulls a pin and causes the wheels to seize up, preventing a runaway trailer.

WALLS AND FRAMING

A teardrop trailer is essentially just a tiny house built on a rolling metal frame, so I decided to follow a similar construction process. The floor, walls, and roof are constructed from 2 x 2 framing. Some basic engineering and common sense is required to build a structure to withstand the stress of traveling 60 miles per hour on the open road. Some builders will argue my framed construction is overkill. Many trailers you see downsize the walls and use just a sheet of ¾-inch-thick plywood and aluminum siding. This reduces the weight a little, and still provides adequate structural support. Just make sure you invest in good quality plywood.

EXTERIOR SIDING

There are many options to consider when designing the exterior. Mine is two-toned, with the top made from carefully resawn redwood covered in an epoxy finish and varnish, and the bottom wrapped in thin-sheet aluminum with plywood sheathing. A wood roof is not a great choice for hot, desert climates so weigh all your options before you follow my lead.

SIDE DOOR

The most common way to provide access to the trailer's main sleeping quarters is a commercially manufactured swinging door. They range in shape and size from

And then there are custom doors, like the two I built for this project. Custom doors give you total control over the design. On the flip side, they give you total responsibility for keeping the water out. For most, watertight doors are a challenge best left to the professionals, and the crazy ones like me.

There are just a few door styles available for teardrop trailers due to the limited size restrictions. The wider variety of RV doors are too tall for most teardrop trailers and are difficult to design around while keeping your trailer well balanced. Do an Internet search for "Teardrop Trailer Passenger's Side Door" and you'll find the familiar-looking insulated face-mount foam core door. This manufactured door comes with a built-in tinted window, vent and screen, exterior key lock, interior dead-bolt lock, and all the required stainless-steel mounting hardware. Just cut out an opening on your trailer wall and it drops right in with easy face-plate mounting instructions. Just like that you've got a weatherproof entry and exit with ventilation and a view!

Handle and hardware

If you chose to build custom doors, there are several online retailers that sell sturdy front-mounting door hinges and solid metal locking door handles in a variety of styles. Purchase these ahead of time so you can incorporate their installation requirements into your design. It's more difficult to fit hardware to a constructed door after the fact.

WINDOWS AND HATCHES

Strategically placed windows can provide natural light and much-needed fresh air inside a trailer. Meanwhile, misplaced windows can turn your tiny trailer into an

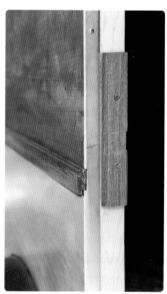

Line the door opening with a threshold and lock plate to keep the water out (left). Here's a look at the completed door (center). A mahogany trim spacer gets the handle to the right position (right top). Align the interior lock with the edge of the door so it overlaps with the door frame when locked (right bottom).

A handmade bug-screen attaches to the opening with hook-and-loop tape (right). The front hatch window provides natural light and ventilation when parked at the campsite (bottom left). A manufactured porthole window provides a picturesque view of your campsite (bottom right).

oven or a leaky ship. Protecting your trailer from weather damage is the number one priority when thinking about windows and hatches. Like doors, the best windows come from commercial manufacturers who have got it right when it comes to weatherproof connections. Still, I decided to make my own front hatch from scratch to achieve my design aspirations.

provide air circulation. There's also a safety precaution: a sealed trailer with vent and windows closed can run out of air in a few hours. Sleep with the vent or windows cracked to ensure fresh air.

REAR HATCH

At the tail end of the trailer a lift-up hatch door opens a galley outfitted with a kitch

A pair of gas-shock props keep the kitchen galley hatch open. When closed, a pair of spring hinges lock it shut.

Hurricane Hinge

These hardy hatch hinges are the go-to option for most custom teardrop trailer builds. They are strong, sturdy, and weather resistant. The unique aluminum extrusion creates a connection with no mechanical parts, so there's nothing really that can break. Alternatives like piano hinges are more difficult to keep watertight.

Gas-shock props

It's a breeze to raise and lower the heavy hatch door when you install standard gas-shock props on each side. These are just like the lifts you'll find on a pickup truck camper shell or recreational boat. Look for a pair that extends about 20 inches and is rated for about 60 pounds. There are a few other lift hinge designs on the market; consider these if you don't feel like hassling with the complexity of gas-shock props. Alternatively, you can go the super–DIY route: prop your hatch open with a pair of sticks. Just make sure they're

safe. You don't want your door dropping on your head.

GALLEY KITCHEN

The hallmark of a teardrop trailer design is the rear-facing kitchen that's tucked away neatly beneath the hatch. There are countless ways to design and lay out a galley kitchen. I kept mine simple.

Sink basin

Options range from a simple bucket and water jug to a hand-pump system to a high-end plumbing system powered by electricity. I bought a collapsible bucket and cut the countertop to fit.

Cooler box

You'll be the coolest kids at the campground with a proper refrigeration system. Design a convenient spot for a removable cooler box as I did, or go big with a built-in refrigeration system powered by an on-board battery.

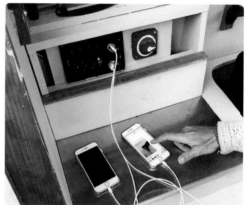

A sink basin, cooler box, and dedicated space for the 12-volt electrical system and interior and exterior lights are simple upgrades that can improve your lifestyle at the campsite.

Pantry cabinets

Plan for plenty of storage to house all your kitchen and camping gear.

Battery box

The galley also is a good place to house the 12-volt electrical system. Mine fits safely in a tidy cubby in the kitchen galley. It's easy to access, but out of the way.

Running lights, brake lights, and blinkers

The minimum requirement for a utility trailer is a 4-pin system, which transfers power from your car battery to the trailer's brake lights, running lights, and blinkers. I upgraded to a 7-pin system, which adds additional power lines to the

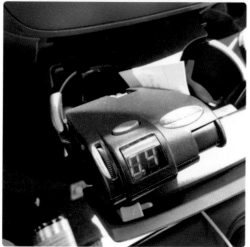

Hanging storage bags, electric brakes, and electric running lights add functionality to the trailer.

These have a built-in accelerometer to measure the deceleration of your tow vehicle and adjust the intensity of the trailer brakes. That way, however you brake your vehicle, the trailer will also brake. You may also find older style "time-delay" brake controllers, which send the same amount of preset power to your trailer brakes every time.

12-volt interior power system

Upgrade your electrical system by installing a deep-cycle marine battery in the trailer to power on-board lights, entertainment devices, and appliances.

I didn't do this, but you can also install a power converter for a 120-volt AC system. Now you can run your TV, mini-fridge, or coffee maker. Add photovoltaic panels for sun-powered battery charging, and living off the grid is a real possibility.

Light fixtures and switches

Purchase all the electrical supplies and light fixtures from a marine parts store, specialty trailer store, or online retailer. For the exterior lighting, I purchased marine-rated lights that are designed to stay waterproof under intense wind and rain conditions.

Inspired by a surfboard

I once built a hollow wooden surfboard. The construction process is nearly 100 years old, invented by a Wisconsin-born swimmer named Tom Blake.

Recently, the process has been revived by several makers around the globe who produce beautifully shaped surfboards and offer mail-order kits and hands-on workshops. I built one on my own, following plans from a Maine-based company called Grain Surfboards. When it came time to design my trailer, that surfboard served as great inspiration.

The first idea was the material selection—old-grown redwood and cedar with the grain running in a straight, quarter-sawn orientation.

The second inspiration was the construction technique—a strong but lightweight method of creating a curvy 3-D form. Inside is a center spine cut from plywood and a series of shaped ribs that run the entire length, kind of like those dinosaur models you may have built as a kid. The skeleton parts connect with half-lap joints and a dab of wood glue. Then, it all gets locked into place with a thin wood skin on all sides. As it turns out, it's also a good technique for building the wall and roof structure of a trailer.

With the lumber milled to thickness, the edges are jointed to create near-invisible seams when assembled edge to edge.

Make a plan

Compared with the many builds I studied, the way I imagined my build going together was slightly different. Rather than building the exterior body of the trailer first, and then outfitting the inside with cabinetry and details, my process flipped the order of construction. After building a sturdy platform base, I constructed the trailer from the inside out, starting with the interior walls and cabinetry, then the framing, then the exterior skin.

I've never been one for following instructions (though I do enjoy giving them), so I didn't make an official set of "plans." Instead, I created rough measured drawings and construction details to guide me through the process.

This approach leaves some breathing room for on-the-spot decisions that lead to stronger, more reliable construction, or a faster way to complete a process. Finally, not being wedded to a plan

Sketchbook:
MEASURED DRAWINGS

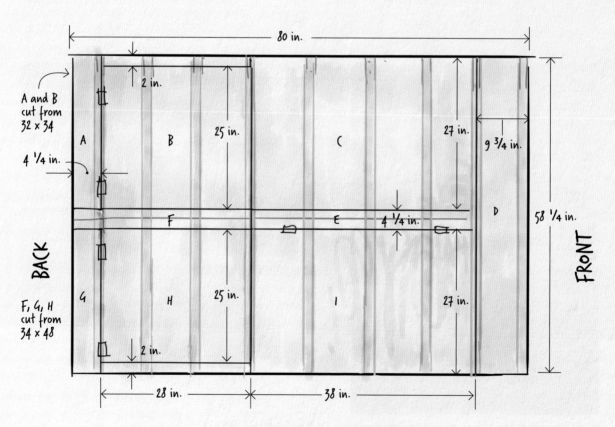

BED FRAME with STORAGE

makes it easier to absorb your mistakes. When you make a bad cut or decision, you won't feel so bad about scrapping your plan.

Basically, what I'm trying to say is that my "plans" didn't end up the way they started. I drew in layers, adding new ones through various stages of construction, adjusting dimensions to reality—and mistakes—along the way. (I'll point out when that happens, and how to fix it.)

This collection of drawings is specific to my trailer, but you should consider the measurements and features malleable. Adapt them for your own needs. In fact, I encourage you to veer from this design and build a teardrop trailer that fulfills your wildest imagination in style, form, and function.

WIRED for TRAVEL

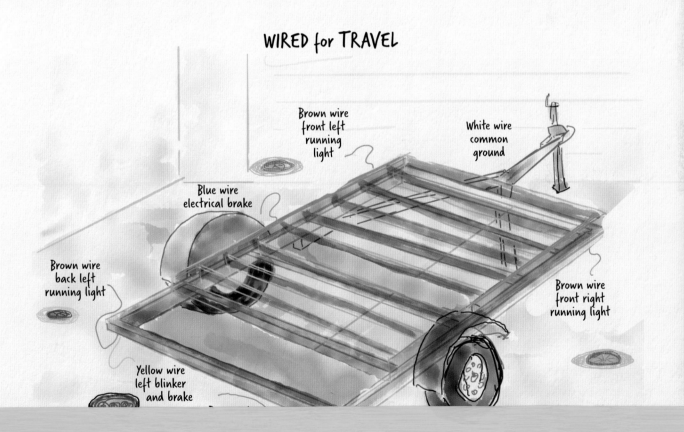

Brown wire front left running light

White wire common ground

Blue wire electrical brake

Brown wire back left running light

Brown wire front right running light

Yellow wire left blinker and brake

Sketchbook:
MEASURED DRAWINGS (CONTINUED)

← Center door section

Cut from sheet 56 in. tall by 48 in. wide

← Galley kitchen section

Cut from sheet 56 in. tall by 44 in. wide

Door opening 27 1/2 in. wide by 42 in. tall

Front headboard section

Cut from sheet 48 in. tall by 14 in. wide

INTERIOR WALLS

KITCHEN BUILT-INS

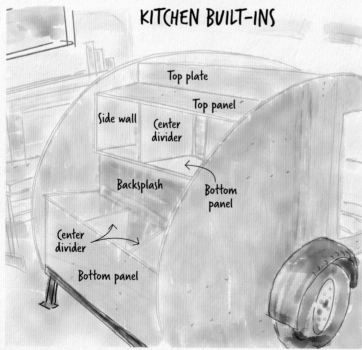

Top plate

Top panel

Side wall

Center divider

Backsplash

Bottom panel

Center divider

Bottom panel

KITCHEN HATCH

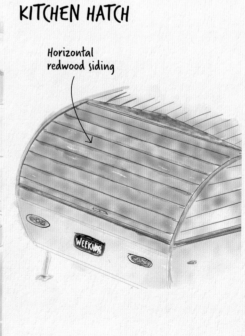

Horizontal redwood siding

WEEKNDR

Sketchbook:
MEASURED DRAWINGS (CONTINUED)

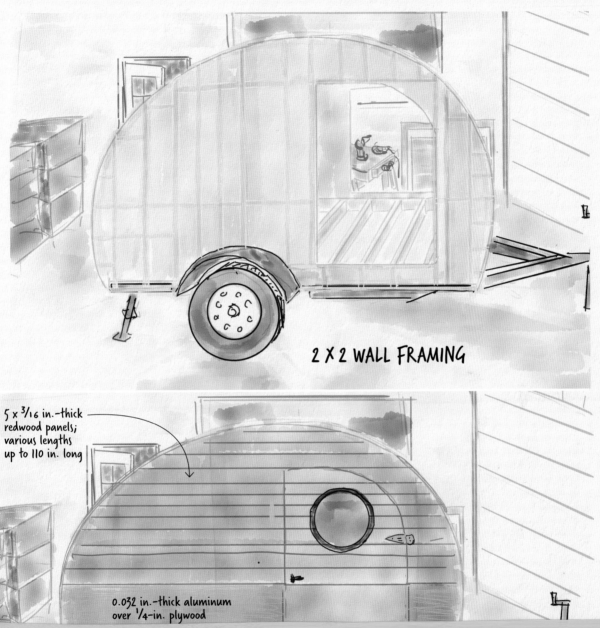

2 X 2 WALL FRAMING

5 x 3/16 in.-thick redwood panels; various lengths up to 110 in. long

0.032 in.-thick aluminum over 1/4-in. plywood

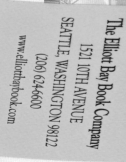

WHAT YOU'LL NEED

12 x 5 x 8-ft. custom utility trailer with:

- 15-in. wheels
- Electric brakes
- Torsion suspension
- (2) rear support stands
- Trailer wiring for lights, brakes, and battery
- Steel fenders
- State registration
- Van hitch and electrical installation (2-in. ball hitch with 7-pin connectors and brake controller)

Sheet Goods

- (2) ¾-in. 4 x 8-ft. exterior plywood sheets (Platform)
- (1) ¾-in. 4 x 8-ft. finished plywood sheet (Bed box)
- (7) ½-in. 4 x 8-ft. finished plywood sheets (Interior walls, shelves, and flooring)
- (3) ¾-in. 4 x 8-ft. finished plywood sheets (Galley cabinetry and hatch ribs)
- (1) ¼-in. 4 x 8-ft. finished plywood sheet (Cabinet back and upholstered headboard)
- (2) ¼-in. 4 x 8-ft. exterior plywood sheets (Exterior sheathing)
- (3) 10 ft. x 30 in. x .032-in. aluminum sheets (Exterior siding)
- (1) roll floor foam underlayment
- (2) 1 ½-in. 4 x 8-ft. sheets rigid foam insulation

Lumber

- (12) 8-ft.-long 2 x 4s (Trailer frame to platform connection)
- (24) 8-ft.-long redwood 2 x 2s (Rafter framing)

- (30) 8-ft.-long pine 2 x 2s (Wall and door post framing)
- (2) 120 x 1 ½ x ¼-in. Alaskan yellow cedar (Top plate)
- (13) 110 x 6 x 3/16-in. cedar (Interior panels)
- (12) 48 x 2 x ⅛-in. maple veneer (Door edging and fender templates)
- (30) 110 x 6 x 3/16-in. redwood (Exterior top, side, and hatch panels)
- (8) 8-ft. x 2 x ¾-in. mahogany (Rear hatch crossbeams)
- (2) 10-ft. x ¼ x ¼-in. redwood trim bead
- 60 ft. extruded aluminum trim (various shapes and profiles)
- (4) 8-ft. x 2 ½ x ⅝-in. mahogany trim (Trim, hatch handle, light plates, license plate frame)

Adhesives

- Contractor's adhesive
- Wood glue (such as Titebond III)
- Marine adhesive (such as 3M Fast Cure 5200)
- Contact cement
- Silicone adhesive

Finishing Materials

- 1 ½ gallon pack 2-part epoxy (such as Entropy Resins from West Systems)
- 1 pint exterior polyurethane finish (exterior)
- 1 pint exterior paint (Kitchen galley cabinets)

Upholstery

- (1) rolled queen-size mattress (such as Ikea)

- 3 yds fabric (upholstery)
- 3 yds muslin
- (6) 24 x 12 x 1 ½-in. cushion foam
- Hook-and-loop tape

Electrical

- 4-circuit breaker
- Deep cycle marine battery
- (1) main power switch
- (1) 14-in. 12-volt roof fan
- Interior and exterior light fixtures
- On/off switches
- 14-gauge wire
- (2) red travel lights
- (2) orange travel lights
- (2) rear blinker/brake lights
- (1) license plate light

Hardware

- (20) 2 ½ x 5/16-in. lag bolts
- Screws: #10 1 ⅝-in.; #10 ¾-in.; 1 ½-in.; ⅞-in.; #9 2 ½-in.; 1 ¾-in.; 2-in.; 3-in.
- 1-in. brad nails
- ½-in. staples
- (2) 48-in. T-tracks
- (12) various T-bolts with handles
- (2) 48-in. piano hinges
- (4) flat folding handles
- (12) standard hinges (Headboard)
- (2) Hurricane Hinges (Rear hatch and front window)
- (2) 60-lb. gas-shock props
- (3) door handle and lock sets
- (4) stainless steel "ice box" door hinges
- (2) 12-in. round aluminum-framed porthole windows

Trailer Accessories

- Cooler
- Collapsible sink basin
- Propane camp stove

Tools and Supplies

- (1) sheet 2-in.-thick foam insulation (Sacrificial cutting board)
- 6-ft. story stick
- Safety equipment
- Straightedge
- Clamps
- Circular saw
- Measuring tape
- Drill/driver
- Painter's tape
- Permanent marker
- Random orbit disc sander with a variety of grits
- Jigsaw
- Pencil
- Mitersaw
- Handplanes
- Sanding block
- Utility knife
- Cordless brad nailer
- Bandsaw (optional)
- Jointer/planer (optional)
- Tablesaw or chopsaw (optional)
- Foam brush
- Handsaws
- Staple gun
- Surform rasp
- Carpenter's square
- Pliers
- Chisel
- Mallet
- Handheld trim router
- Wire cutter/stripper
- Lighter
- Paint roller
- Plastic dropcloth
- Epoxy mixing buckets
- Squeegee
- Paintbrushes
- Rubber gloves
- Mixing sticks
- Cotton rags

BUY THE HARDWARE AHEAD OF TIME

Before you go too far down the path of cutting lumber and assembling the parts, take a break to order all the parts and accessories that you'll need throughout the project: indoor and outdoor lights, door hinges and hardware, and electronics. These parts will be critical during construction to determine the position of the trailer framing on all sides. Buy these before you get started to ensure that everything fits.

You want to make room for mechanics and moving parts, but also install blocking so there's a place to mount screws and bolts.

LESSONS LEARNED

Before you embark on my guided journey, let me make this disclosure: You will see mistakes made, and solutions discovered. For example, despite the strong words of advice from experienced builders I met along the way, I opted not to use manufactured doors and windows, but rather designed and built my own from scratch. This decision added a lot of complexity, time, and cost to my project, and the likelihood of water intrusion down the road is high. Throughout the book you'll hear me explain more of these lessons learned and suggest easy alternative materials or construction techniques that you might consider for your build.

All said and done, these "mistakes" are mostly in my imagination. Those who pass by me on the highway or park nearby at the campsite will never know. And despite all my stubborn compromises, the result is a one-of-a-kind trailer that I'm excited to enjoy and maintain for years to come.

Oh yeah, the question I know you're dying to get answered because everyone always asks: How long did it take?

Realistically, expect to invest about 200 to 300 hours into your first build. If you worked 8 hours a day straight, maybe you could finish in three or four weeks.

My build took a lot longer for a few reasons. I wanted to make sure I didn't pass on bad information to readers so I did a lot of research and overthinking at each step. I also was taking photos, drawing illustrations, and writing the book along the way, so that slowed me down. Not to mention, I had a day job and was working mostly nights and weekends.

My best piece of advice to you is don't give yourself any deadlines and take the time to do it right. Once your trailer's built, there will be plenty of time to enjoy it (and make modifications).

I bet you're also wondering: How much did it cost?

I kept a log of every purchase and related expenses like new tools and supplies, and my total cost of goods—drum roll please—was $6,771.75.

I overbought a few expensive items, not knowing my exact needs up front. And I selected premium materials in some cases where I could have downgraded to save a lot of money. So there's plenty of room to reduce the budget on your build.

Ten Questions
ON CHOOSING A TRAILER

The moment arrived when it was time to start building my trailer and spending money on materials and parts. The first purchase is the big one: the trailer frame that will support the tiny camper on top.

The trailer frame, the hitch, the axle, the wheels: these are the bones of your vehicle and not the place to skimp. Don't be tempted by low-priced trailers that ship in a box and bolt together. These are not a good choice in terms of safety and longevity.

Another option is to build your own trailer, welding together steel framing and outfitting it with all the parts. But that option was way outside my comfort zone. Not to mention, starting with a bolt-together trailer or building your own from the ground up will make it more difficult to get the finished teardrop trailer licensed for the road.

So, after determining my general measurements—a 5 x 8-foot bed—I took my scratch plans to the nearest trailer yard for some help.

My trip to the trailer lot

My local trailer lot is a flat dusty lot at the intersection of a major highway and a major surface road. I looked around for the friendliest associate who would go easy on a know-nothing like me, but made eye contact with a guy who appeared to be the boss. I stumbled through my idea—to build a teardrop trailer on top of a manufactured utility trailer—and asked if this was something he could help me with. With a low growl, he motioned for me to go on.

I first inquired about the stock utility trailers on the lot, all wired up and ready to drive. Could I start with one of those?

I don't remember his exact reply, but it was something like "You could, but I wouldn't." He explained that a stock trailer off the lot would have features I didn't need—like raised steel railings and a tailgate—and were missing key features that I would need.

For the next 15 minutes I coaxed the basic decisions I would need to resolve before he could write up an order and take my money.

Question #1:

How much weight do you plan to tow?

There's a reason this question comes first. For the sake of your vehicle's health, the first thing you need to know is the maximum weight your vehicle can tow. Manufacturers provide this information in the car specs as "maximum towing capacity." If you exceed it, you are likely to void your vehicle's warranty—and probably screw up the transmission. Most cars and vans with six cylinders have a towing capacity of 2,500 pounds to 3,500 pounds. So, I set my target weight to top out at the lower end of that scale.

In order to not exceed the towing capacity, you must consider the entire load of the vehicle when traveling. Start with the weight of the passengers: on average, two adults and two kids weigh about 500 pounds. Next, add 400 pounds for your provisions, luggage, and gear. Now, account for the trailer building materials, roughly 600 pounds of wood, aluminum, insulation, glue, and finish. Finally, add the trailer frame and wheels, roughly 1,000 pounds. Just like that, you've hit the 2,500 pounds limit.

The towing weight also helps determine what size ball hitch you'll need. The boss recommended a 2-inch ball hitch, not too big for its tow weight and not too small.

Not too big, not too small. A 5 x 8-foot bed with a 4-foot tongue pairs great with my family minivan.

Question #2:

What size frame?

When you custom order a trailer frame, you have complete control over its dimension and the placement of all its details and parts. If your design is really unique you may end up with very specific dimensions and details. I decided to design my trailer around a standard 5 x 8-foot trailer frame. It's wide enough for a queen-size bed and long enough to fit a functional tailgate kitchen. Narrowing the trailer frame would mean downsizing to a smaller mattress size. Going up in width would mean taking up more of the traffic lane—not something I wanted to deal with on my first trailer towing experience.

Trailer frame dimensions don't account for the tongue section of the trailer up front or the wheels and fenders on each side, which means the overall footprint of your trailer is bigger. The tongue section up front is an additional 4 feet, bringing the total length of the trailer to 12 feet, bumper to hitch. In retrospect, I would have extended this by another 2 feet to accommodate more towing space up front. This would have been a great place to install a rack to carry the family bikes.

Question #3:

Steel or aluminum?

I ride a bike to work most days and when I went shopping for my road bike, the sales rep explained that steel is the best material for commuter road riding. It absorbs the dips, bumps, and hazards of city roads much better than aluminum, which is stiff and rigid. I applied that same philosophy to my trailer choice. Also, 90 percent of the trailers on the boss's lot were made from steel, so I assumed there was a reason for that. The boss agreed.

Depending on the size and weight of your trailer, you have a few options in the type of steel used in the trailer construction. After looking around the lot at the other trailers, my first instinct was tubular steel. The boss told me that, based on the weight I planned to tow, I could downgrade the frame to U-frame steel or even one step lower, angle iron.

After doing the math I decided to compromise on strength and weight: tubular steel for the frame and angle iron for the four crossbeams equally spaced along the length of the trailer.

Question #4:

What's your wheel size?

Again, looking around the lot, the best trailers were outfitted with full-sized 15-inch road wheels. They just look good. I also learned through my research that the bigger the wheel, the more cushioned the ride. Finally, this size provides a few critical inches of clearance, making the trailer more versatile in where it can travel. The boss told me I could trim a few dollars off the price tag by downsizing to a 14-inch wheel; I could even get away with a 13-inch. Any less, he said, should be avoided.

Question #5:

Brakes or no brakes?

When you're humming down the interstate, and surprised by unexpected traffic—or worse, a deer!—you'll be thankful that you installed electric brakes. Modern-day trailer brakes and brake controls make it easy to operate your trailer brakes safely and reliably in a variety of situations from heavy-duty emergency braking to slowing down at a stop sign.

With a proportional brake controller, a built-in accelerometer measures the deceleration of your tow vehicle and then adjusts the intensity of the trailer brakes and the rate at which they are applied. So, if you slam on the brakes, your trailer brakes will activate with that same extreme intensity. And if you steadily slow down as you approach a stop, your trailer will gradually brake in the same manner.

Compare that to the older time-delay brake controllers, which send the same amount of preset power to your trailer brakes every time (hit the brakes and the wheels seize up), and you can understand the benefits to the modern-day upgrade.

An added benefit of installing electric brakes is the addition of the brake chain. It attaches to your vehicle at one end and to the brake box at the other. If your trailer comes unhitched while driving, it pulls a pin from the brake box that immediately seizes the brakes and sets them to locked mode—preventing a runaway trailer.

Question #6:
What kind of suspension?

The stock utility trailers found on most commercial lots come with standard leaf-spring suspension. You'd recognize these even if you don't know much about automobile mechanics. These U-shaped metal arches attach to the axle and frame, and absorb bumps and dips as you drive. Upgrade from the stock leaf-spring suspension to torsional suspension for an even softer ride down the highway. This system relies on a rubber-cushioned steel tube that absorbs road shock, improves road handling, and reduces trailer sway. This added luxury (and

safety) comes at a cost: $299 plus tax as of this writing.

Question #7:
How about the trailer lights?

I assumed that any trailer I ordered would come with the basic blinkers and brake lights that make it road legal. I was wrong. I had to specify to the boss that I wanted this pre-installed. He explained that this step is usually left until the final stages of the build. But electrical was not my expertise so I asked him to install as much as they could without impacting my build. It was a good decision because it turns out that the placement of the trailer road lights is what the Department of Motor Vehicles is most concerned with.

In addition to the required lights, I also wired a line to charge the on-board battery when driving.

With all this installed, the trailer requires a 7-pin cable to connect to your vehicle. Without the brakes and battery charging, you can downsize to a 4-pin connection.

Question #8:

Fenders before or after?

Oh, and how about fenders? I could install those now or later, the boss explained. But choosing to install them later would give me more flexibility in my construction. I didn't listen and chose to have them welded to the trailer frame before delivery. In retrospect, I should have listened to his advice and purchased them on the side to install after the walls were framed and built. It would have made it much easier to complete the waterproofing where the walls meet the fenders. And by the time I finished the build, they had been dinged up enough that they had to be sanded down and re-painted.

Question #9:

Anything else?

One day while visiting a nearby neighborhood I spotted a teardrop trailer parked in front of a home. I noticed two retractable legs that folded up and stored underneath when the trailer was not in use, and folded down when parked. I'll take two of those, I told the boss.

Other features to consider in retrospect are a retractable step welded below the location of the side doors for easier entry, and a metal storage box with spare tire mount on the front-end trailer tongue.

Question #10:

How soon do you need it?

Based on my answers to the nine questions above, I had designed a unique trailer that would need to be built to spec by the manufacturer. Most dealers won't have your unique combination of needs in stock on the lot. But they can usually order one for delivery in six weeks. In 2016, at the San Francisco Bay area's inflated prices, I dropped about $2,000 for my built-to-order trailer frame, including taxes, registration with the California DMV, and delivery from the factory to the lot. Your price will vary depending on your region and dealer.

Sketchbook:
TRAILER SPECIFICATIONS

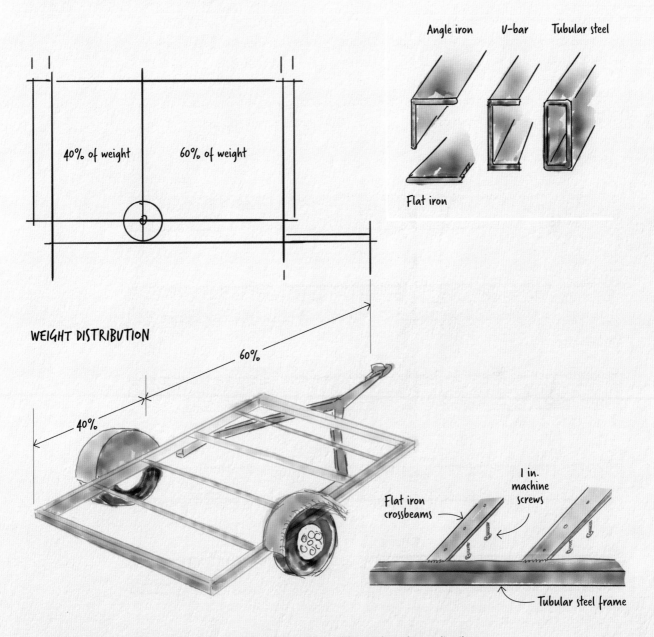

Angle iron   V-bar   Tubular steel

Flat iron

40% of weight   60% of weight

WEIGHT DISTRIBUTION

60%

40%

Flat iron crossbeams

1 in. machine screws

Tubular steel frame

Calculating the location of the axle is not an exact science. The end goal is to distribute 40% of the weight behind the axle and 60% in front. The challenge is that the weight of the metal trailer frame and the trailer on top isn't evenly distributed. The kitchen galley adds extra weight to the tailgate side and the curve of the trailer requires more building materials up front. After doing some fuzzy math, I ended up positioning the axles slightly closer to the front hitch than the mathematical 40/60 point. Additional balancing and fine-tuning can be done when you load your trailer with gear.

Construct a
STURDY BASE

The foundation for my teardrop trailer comes in the form of a plywood platform and raised bed box that attaches firmly to the steel trailer frame. With it secured soundly in place, all the other trailer parts bolt to it, creating an ultra-rigid and sturdy structure.

The bed box is constructed much like a framed wall of a house and creates a rigid structure that serves as a solid mount for the walls and cabinetry. A row of 2 x 4s attach to two side plates on each side that match up with end plates at the front and back, creating rigid box frame.

The shape and height of the bed box is a fun place to mess around with your custom design. I opted for a shallow bed frame to maximize the headroom for campers inside. The 2 x 4 framing gives it just enough room to fill with insulation or use as a shallow storage space. Building the box taller would have allowed for more storage underneath the mattress. I also built the bed box to accommodate side access door.

4.1
Trailer as workbench

In my garage workshop, which I share with the family storage, space is at a premium— especially workshop space. So, I used my trailer frame as a 5 x 8-foot workbench where I could cut and assemble parts on a level surface.

I didn't make this trick up, but I embraced it: lay down a sheet of foam insulation board to use as a sacrificial cutting surface for ripping and cross-cutting plywood. Set the blade height on your circular saw to just over the thickness of the material; as you make the cut, the saw blade will extend into the foam by about ¼-inch.

To guide my circular saw on a straight line, I made a long fence from a 2 x 4 that easily clamps to the workpiece. A stop block is attached at one end at a perfect 90° angle and is marked to identify the location of the blade. To prepare for your cut, set the fence on the workpiece and line up the stop block at the near end. Check your measurements at both ends, then clamp the fence in place.

The goal here is to cover the metal trailer frame edge to edge with exterior plywood, so your dimensions will match the trailer dimensions

Note: I missed a key step by not applying a waterproof barrier to the underside of the trailer platform before assembly. There are two easy ways I could have accomplished this: apply a thick coat of epoxy to the underside of the plywood or lay down a sheet of aluminum first.

1. Make a sacrificial foam cutting board.
Lay down a sheet of at least 2-inch-thick foam insulation and it becomes a nice flat cutting surface for your circular saw. Set the blade to cut about ¼-inch deep into the foam, giving it just enough clearance to cut through your sheet goods and into the foam board.

2. Use a 2 x 4 rip fence.

To rip and cross-cut in a perfectly straight line right where you want, clamp a 2 x 4 down so the circular saw fence can ride against it as you cut.

3. Position the cut.

On my saw, the blade measures exactly 1½ inches from the edge of the fence. So, I clamped the 2 x 4 that distance away from the cutting line.

4. Cut to the line.

Next, push the circular saw steadily along the fence for the entire length of the cut. Let the blade do the work; you're just there to guide it in the right direction.

5. Continue the cut.

For best results, use a straight and square 2 x 4 with a smooth edge for your fence to ride against.

Sketchbook:
A SOLID FOUNDATION

A platform with a wood-framed bed box attaches to the steel trailer frame, providing a solid foundation for the rest of the trailer to be built on and bolted to. Here are a few sketches that detail the construction and assembly.

TRAILER FRAME TO PLATFORM CONNECTION

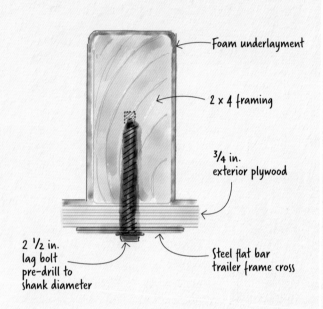

Foam underlayment

2 x 4 framing

3/4 in. exterior plywood

2 1/2 in. lag bolt pre-drill to shank diameter

Steel flat bar trailer frame cross

PLYWOOD CROSSCUT JIG

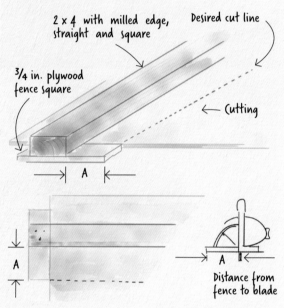

2 x 4 with milled edge, straight and square

Desired cut line

3/4 in. plywood fence square

Cutting

A

A

Distance from fence to blade

PLATFORM AND BED BOX ASSEMBLY

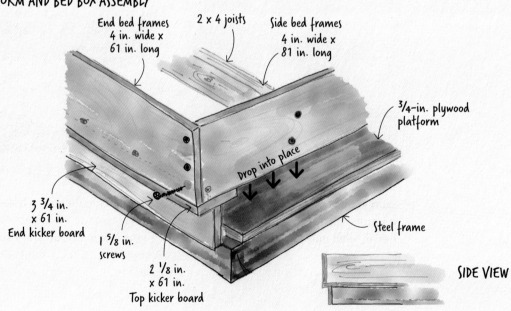

End bed frames 4 in. wide x 61 in. long

2 x 4 joists

Side bed frames 4 in. wide x 81 in. long

3/4-in. plywood platform

Drop into place

Steel frame

3 3/4 in. x 61 in. End kicker board

1 5/8 in. screws

2 1/8 in. x 61 in. Top kicker board

SIDE VIEW

4.2
Glue, screw, lag, and bolt

I don't want to take any chances with my connection, so the plywood panel is attached to the trailer frame with a combination of contractor's cement, sheet metal screws, and heavy-duty bolts.

The first step is to lay out and mark the location of the holes in the steel frame for all your screws and bolts. Then cut each hole with a metal-cutting drill bit. Apply slow steady pressure to the bit as you cut, and wear eye protection. The metal dust and shavings are sharp and may blow around during this operation: keep them out of your eyes.

1. Mark out the hole pattern with a story stick.
With your plywood parts cut to size, now it's time to locate all the holes to be drilled. Apply tape to the steel frame and mark out all the holes. I've never been one for measuring things, that's why I love a good story stick. It's a piece of wood that contains all the measurements and marks. Use it to transfer the hole-cutting pattern to each of the angle-iron cross members.

2. Drill the holes.

Use a drill bit designed for cutting through sheet metal to pilot drill all the holes in the angle-iron. Drill for the #10 sheet metal screws and the 5/16-inch-diameter lag bolts.

3. Lather it with construction adhesive.

Apply contractor's cement to the entire flat surface of the trailer frame where the plywood will rest. Sand down the entire surface with a 60-grit sanding disc to scuff up the surface for better adhesion.

4. Place the plywood on top.
Now place the exterior plywood on top so it rests square and even with all the edges. Position it in place for clamps.

5. Clamp and hold it down.
Apply clamps to the perimeter of the platform to hold the plywood in place as the cement dries.

6. Add weight to the center.
Where your clamps can't reach, place heavy objects to hold down the plywood flat against the steel. A 25-pound anvil comes in handy.

4.3

Build a framed bed box

The platform is now firmly attached to the trailer frame, but for safety's sake, I wanted an additional mechanical connection to ensure that the trailer body sticks firmly to the trailer frame. On top of the platform, I built a raised bed box that plays a functional role in construction and in sleeping.

The bed box is constructed much liked a framed wall on a house, with 2 x 4s spaced 8 inches apart along the length of the trailer frame. Every other 2 x 4 is positioned above the angle-iron trailer frame and a bolt is driven through the steel, then the plywood, and finally into the 2 x 4, creating a bombproof connection to the steel frame.

1. Cut the parts of the bed box.
Cut 4-inch-wide strips from the ¾-inch sheet of plywood.

2. Position the crosscut fence.

Use the platform with a foam panel on top as a cutting table to rip and cross-cut the parts.

3. Cross-cut all the parts at once.

Line up all the bed box parts and cross-cut them all at once with the circular saw. This cut is known as a "gang cut."

4. Assemble the bed box on top.

Use a scrap block of wood to align the parts square at each corner. Then glue and screw the parts.

5. Position the floor joists.

Cross-cut six 2 x 4s to fit inside the bed box. These are positioned over each of the steel angle-iron crossbars. Apply construction adhesive and clamp them in place while you lock them in with screws.

6. Attach from underneath.

Lock it in place with #10 x ¾-inch sheet metal screws. Drive them through the angle iron and into the plywood from underneath.

7. Lag it in place.

Drive ⁵⁄₁₆-inch lag bolts through the angle iron and plywood into the 2 x 4 crossbeams.

Build the
INTERIOR CABINETRY

Constructing the body of a teardrop trailer is a daunting task. The sheer size of each wall and the continuous curve can make it feel undoable for a DIY builder at home in the garage. At least that's how I felt, having never built anything bigger than a queen-size bed. To overcome the scale, I took a unique construction approach that could be easily managed by two hands alone. I built it from the inside out, starting with the inside walls, and also divided the body into three smaller sections that are assembled in manageable parts.

At the tailgate end of the teardrop trailer, a galley with kitchen cabinets, pantry storage, and kitchen utilities provides a solid base to secure the body on the trailer bed.

The center section of the trailer body is much simpler. Two walls and a roof overhead accommodate a door on each side and a ceiling fan on top to vent and cool the inside.

The final section of the trailer is a headboard and cabinet. Above that, a small hatch opens to reveal a tent window to let in fresh air and the view.

Sketchbook:
CABINETRY CONSTRUCTION

Each sidewall is cut from three sheets of ½-inch birch plywood oriented vertically. The cabinet cases take two sheets of ¾-inch birch plywood and serve as the primary lateral support. Once assembled, the cabinet boxes mount to the walls with glue and screws, and each section straddles the base and attaches with screws and glue.

SIDE PANELS

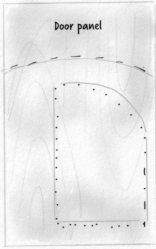

Kitchen panel · Door panel · Front panel

8 ft.

4 ft.

CABINET CASES

JOINERY

WALL-TO-BASE CONNECTION

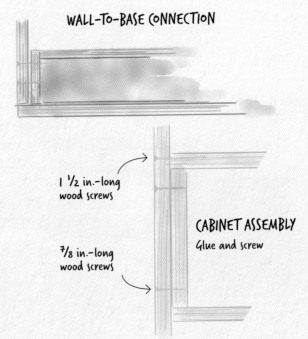

1 ½ in.-long wood screws

7/8 in.-long wood screws

CABINET ASSEMBLY
Glue and screw

5.1

Measuring and cutting the side panel curve

My wife and I own a minivan and a hatchback, so my access to big pieces of lumber is limited to the standard 4 x 8-foot sheet of plywood available at the nearest big box home store. That's not big enough to accommodate the dimensions of my trailer walls, which are oversize by another foot in each direction; this makes it impossible to create each wall out of a single sheet of plywood. If you can find a lumberyard that sells oversized sheet goods, then you're in luck. Cut each side from one of those and save yourself some time. But if you're like me and buy your sheet goods from the local home center, the side panels can be divided into three sections and combined to make up the continuous curve from tailgate to hitch.

Each section makes up a portion of the trailer's curved profile. To draw the curve, I looked to nature rather than computer-aided design. Using a long thin strip of cedar, I created a natural arc by bending it from end to end and clamping it in place. The curve won't be perfectly repeatable, but you can fine-tune the exact curve and eyeball it until you get it just right. As you move to the next panel, take the measurement from where the first curve ends and mark that point on the second panel. Then clamp the cedar strip at that point and continue the curve. Repeat the process a third time to complete the curve at the hitch end of the trailer.

Dry fit all the parts and check your work from a few different angles. If the curve looks off, remove additional materials until it's just right.

1

2

3

4

1. Create naturally perfect curves.
The thin strips of cedar that will be used for siding and roof serve as a great tool for drawing a fair and even curve on the side panel sections.

2. Set each end and bend.
Clamp one end of the cedar strip at the beginning of your curve.

3. Get creative with clamping.
Establish the long curve and then clamp the other end of the cedar strip in place.

4. Mark the cut.
When you're happy with the curve, trace the edge pencil to establish your cut line.

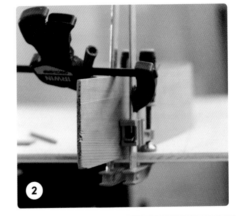

5. Cut to the line.
Cut the curved edge with a jigsaw. Go slow and steady and keep and equal distance from the pencil line for a clean cut.

6. Leave a notch.
The bottom of each panel on the kitchen cabinet section is cut out to leave a small point at the end so the teardrop curve can continue all the way to the bottom edge of the bumper.

7. Clean up the edges by hand.
Clean up the edges with a block plane or sanding block to prevent splinters.

8. Continue the curve.

Move on to the center panel side walls and continue the curve. Mark the distance from the bottom at each end of the curve and use the cedar strip to establish a fair and elegant shape.

9. Cut to the line.

Draw a line for the jigsaw cut and continue the process for the final headboard section on each side.

10. Take a look.

Test fit the wall panels and behold your final curve!

11. Temporarily secure.

Temporarily hold each panel in place with a clamp so you can view it from different angles.

12. Make the matching sides.
When you like your shape, transfer each panel to the matching panel on the opposite side.

13. History is your guide.
Cut the matching panel with a jigsaw. I was brave enough to use the already-cut side to guide my saw blade, but if you don't have the same confidence, mark the edge with a pencil line.

14. Use a block plane to perfect the edge.
Hand tools offer a quiet and accurate method to fair the curve and maintain the 90° edge. Use a power sander for a dustier, louder approach.

5.2
A tidy kitchen adds strength

The bulk of the structural support for the trailer comes from the framing and kitchen cabinetry. When you glue and screw the plywood boxes to the side walls, it provides great torsional support to keep the trailer from swaying side-to-side. The cabinets also provide storage for all your gear, and workspaces for prepping and cooking. I designed mine to be simple, but this is where you should let your imagination and ambition run wild. Design your galley kitchen to meet your needs.

I followed the most common layout, with the pantry and base cabinets divided into thirds. Deep and tall dimensions make it versatile for packing all your cold and pantry food, cooking gear (even the coffee maker), kitchen utilities, and the heavy stuff like ice and water.

Use the flat foundation of the trailer as a workbench to assemble the cabinets. Start with the base cabinet, then proceed to the pantry cabinet. Install at a height that does not interfere with the hatch door when closed—at least 3 inches from the wall edge. I installed mine 2 inches too high, complicating the hatch installation later on.

①

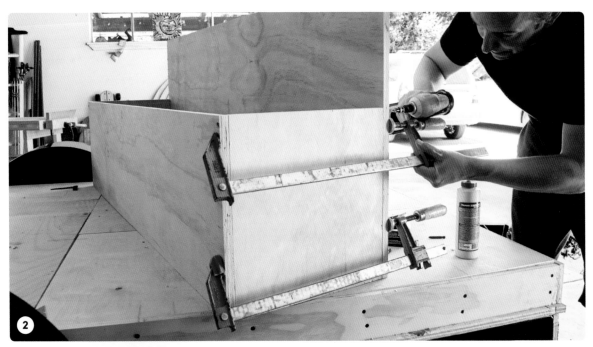

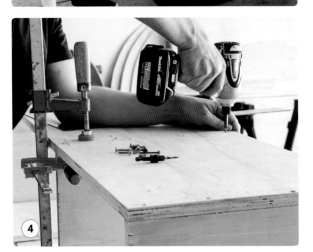

1. Prep the cabinet parts.
Cut all the cabinet parts with a circular saw and straightedge. Then, assemble the kitchen cabinet box with wood glue and screws.

2. Move on to the next one.
Continue assembling each corner with the same method.

3. Position the center dividers.
Measure equidistant from each edge to install two center dividers to create three sections: sink, cooler, and utilities.

4. Secure the dividers.
Divide the box into three equal sections. Then clamp and screw them into place.

BUILD THE INTERIOR CABINETRY

A tidy kitchen adds strength

5. Watch the tailgate take shape.
Attach the side panels to the cabinet and your trailer really starts to take shape!

6. Dry-fit for reference.
Place the center panels back on the trailer to ensure alignment on the curved edge where the two panels join.

7. Set everything in place.
Apply wood glue and then screw the side panels to the center cabinet and bed frame at the base.

8. Get a good, tight fit.
Set the top cabinet box in place and apply glue to the sides where they join to the wall. Hold the cabinets temporarily with clamps, and screw into place with ⅞-inch-long wood screws. (A second pair of hands helps.)

5.3
Build out the headboard

The hitch end of the trailer goes together as a skeleton at this stage of the build. The bare-bones structure is a simple cabinet frame that will later be built out with an upholstered headboard with shallow cabinets. These cabinets serve as ideal places to store flashlights, paperbacks, clocks, pocket knives, and other personal stuff. But don't worry too much about that now; you just want a bare minimum of parts to help the walls line up straight and square.

1. Move along to the front.
The front headboard is assembled from a few barebone parts.

2. Frame a simple shelf.
Measure the top shelf at each end to ensure level alignment and glue and screw the shelf in place.

3. Pause for a look.
Fit in an old queen-size mattress to do a gut check on the design so far.

5.4
Cut out the side entry doors

The center section of the trailer does not contain any cabinetry. The only work here is to cut openings for the side entry doors.

Because my doors are custom made, I was not precise with the measurements and placement of the opening. Just make sure to leave at least 7 inches of material around the opening for strength.

The plywood off-cuts become the foundation for the custom doors later, so take great care when cutting them out to preserve them.

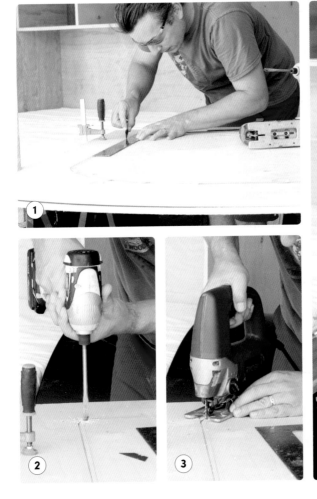

1. Cut out a door.
Measure and mark out the side-door opening on the center panel. Scribe a line along the perimeter with a razor blade to ensure a clean cut with the jigsaw to preserve the door edge.

2. Start with a pilot hole.
Drill a hole in the bottom inside corner of the door opening to fit the jigsaw blade.

3. Start your cut.
Insert the jigsaw blade into the pilot hole to begin the cut. Stay just shy of the inside of the line.

4. Make a handmade straightedge.
When cutting long straight lines, clamp a plywood strip to the workpiece to guide the jigsaw.

5. Go freehand for curves.
Continue the curved section of the door opening with a freehand cut, going slow and steady.

6. Take a good look!
Dry-fit the center panel to check your work.

Frame the
ROOF AND WALLS

With the interior walls up and the kitchen and headboard cabinetry installed, it's time to strengthen the trailer body with framing. This is where the real integrity of the structure comes from. Good framing is what will keep your trailer humming down the highway unfazed at 60 miles per hour.

Start by connecting the two walls with 2 x 2 rafters that span from tailgate to hitch. I set each rafter evenly apart every 5 inches with some additional rafters installed where the trailer needs some extra support—like the plywood seams and the area around the front window and roof vent.

Same goes when framing the side walls. Tall upright 2 x 2s span each side of the trailer, aligned with every other roof rafter. Add extra framing around the areas that need it.

The goal here is to build a solid framework. But don't overbuild it: keep things lightweight.

6.1

Wrap the roof with rafters

I brainstormed ways to establish a strong joint where the rafter meets the walls, but I kept coming back to the simplest approach: fit a 2 x 2 between the two walls with a butt joint and attach them with glue and screws. Additional structural support at the wall-to-roof joint will come during later steps in the process.

I whipped up a simple clamping jig (seen in step 2) to hold the rafters perfectly in place. Just clamp the jig to the side walls on both sides. Set the rafter in place. Measure

and fine-tune the placement, then clamp the rafter to the jig. It's now temporarily secured while you pilot drill the screw hole and add a countersink. This made it easy to install them single handedly without fumbling around or knocking them out of alignment.

Dab a little glue on the joint to hold it in place, then drill and countersink for the screw and drive it home. Continue the process for each rafter, making your way from one end to the other.

①

1. Install the rafters.
Your trailer is starting to take shape. Now it's time to lock it into place with screws and rafters.

2. The clamping jig is your third hand.
Mark the location where the rafter attaches to the wall, then position the clamping jig and secure it in place.

3. Secure the rafter.
Set the 2 x 2 on the clamping jig and secure it in place with a clamp.

4. Clamp it at both ends.
Clamp the rafter in a clamping jig on the opposite side, making sure it's even and square at both ends.

1

2

3

5. Prep the connection.

Drill through the plywood wall and into the end grain of the rafter. Add a countersink so the screw engages firmly and doesn't force the wood to split.

6. Add a drop of glue for good measure.

Wood glue helps lock the rafter in place with a single screw.

7. Secure the rafters with screws.

Drive a 2½-inch long #9 construction-grade screw through the side wall and into the center of the rafter. Continue by spacing each rafter evenly, except to accommodate the front window and the top vent.

5

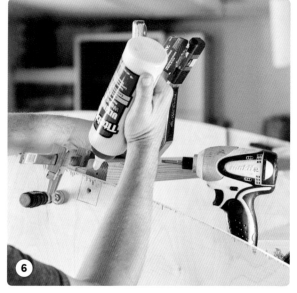
6

7

Sketchbook:
RAFTER JOINERY

The joinery to connect the walls to the roof required a lot of thought. It needs to serve many masters: keep the water out and the framing steady, square, and securely in place. I consulted an architect friend and sketched out the following ideas before building.

RAFTER-TO-WALL JOINERY

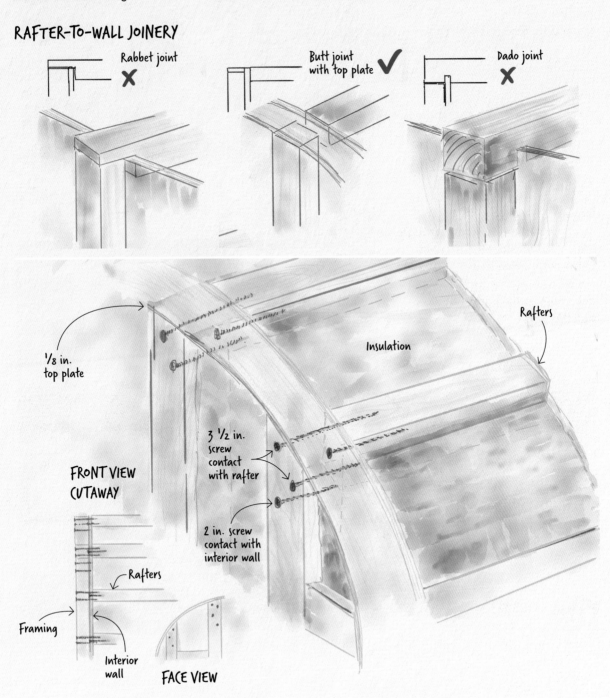

Rabbet joint ✗

Butt joint with top plate ✓

Dado joint ✗

¹/₈ in. top plate

Insulation

Rafters

3 ¹/₂ in. screw contact with rafter

2 in. screw contact with interior wall

FRONT VIEW CUTAWAY

Rafters

Framing

Interior wall

FACE VIEW

6.2

Make room for a roof vent and front window hatch

When you reach the location of the ceiling fan and front window hatch, you'll need to adjust the installation pattern. The rafters don't extend from wall to wall, and need additional support to keep this section from sagging.

To determine your measurements for these short, reinforced sections, use the actual fan to determine the positioning of the roof framing where the top vent will be installed. The model I ordered online fit a standard 14-inch opening.

I was less precise with the dimensions of the front window hatch because I made it from scratch versus using a commercial production and just built it to fit.

After I started construction on the front window hatch, I learned that a front face is the worst place to install a window on a trailer because it faces winds head-on when driving down the highway. This oncoming wind can push water into the tiniest little gap or crack left exposed by

the window mechanics. With that in mind, I tried to engineer my front hatch with extra flashing. Hopefully it will hold up over time. If you're worried about leakage, you can modify it or leave this front window hatch out of your build.

1

1. Attach the short rafters.

Cut and assemble the parts for the small sections of rafters that straddle the roof vent and front window. Cut a curved piece from plywood that matches the curve of the wall, then join it with the two short rafters at the workbench.

2. Fit around the vent.

To ensure a snug fit, temporarily position the ceiling vent between the two rafters with a pair of the clamping jigs described earlier in this chapter.

3. Reinforce the vent.

When the sections are set and aligned, glue and screw them into place.

6 FRAME THE ROOF AND WALLS

Make room for a roof vent and front window hatch

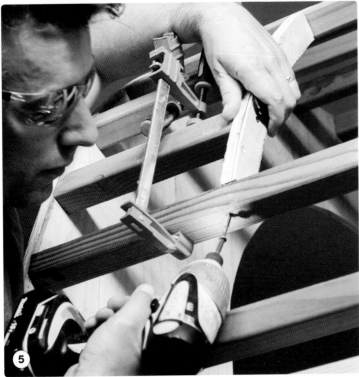

4. Frame the window.
Build up the framing to support the window hatch opening at the front of the trailer.

5. Add vertical support.
Cut two short pieces that match the curve of the trailer to frame the left and right side of the window opening. Use the actual trailer walls as your guides.

6.3

Framing the walls

The wall framing goes together quickly. The goal here is to attach a series of vertical 2 x 2s to the side walls, evenly spaced and aligned with the roof rafters and at each seam where the interior walls join.

Install short pieces horizontally in key locations to serve as blocking and mounting surfaces for later when you attach the outside wall materials. A few primary spots to consider are where you will install the door hardware and hinges, the location of all your lights and electrical fixtures, and at any seam where exterior materials join up.

Installing the framing after the interior walls is an unconventional method that requires an unusual connection. Each 2 x 2 is attached with exterior-grade PVA glue and 1 ¾-inch long wood screws. Keep in mind: a 2 x 2 actually measures 1 ½ inches square, and the thickness of the ½-inch plywood brings the total material thickness to 2 inches. The screw must extend past the 1 ½-inch frame and into the ½-inch plywood without poking through.

For a perfect fit, countersink the screw hole so that the 1 ¾-inch screw sets flush and extends just shy of the plywood outer face.

Finally, install a top plate. This thin and narrow strip of wood wraps around the perimeter of the entire framed wall at the roof and bottom edges. This piece locks all the framed parts together at the ends and acts like the top plate in a framed building wall.

1. Frame the sides for shear strength.

Install the key wall posts where they're needed most: the seams where the wall sections join and the door frames. The wall posts are pine, and the rafters are redwood.

2. Trim each wall post to fit.
Trace the cutting angle where the wall post meets the roofline to custom-fit each piece. You can use the actual wall as a guide, and a bevel gauge to transfer the cutting angle to the miter saw.

3. Add blocking.
Add additional wall posts as needed to prevent a span greater than 8 inches and blocking to install mechanics and hardware.

4. Make room for the top plate.
Use a spacer the thickness of your top plate to set the position of each vertical framing member.

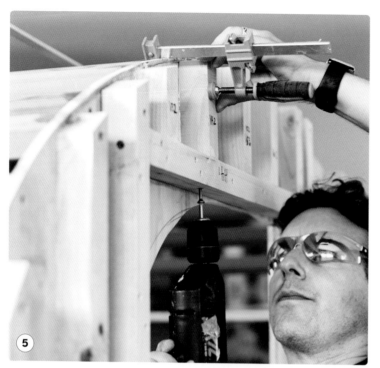

5. Attach the wall posts.

After all the parts are cut to size and dry-fit, clamp the parts with construction adhesive. Pilot drill and countersink a screw hole, then drive home heavy-duty screws—2-inch in general, 3-inch when matching up with a rafter. Aim to make contact with the rafters at the top of each vertical post. Don't allow the screws to protrude through the inside wall.

6. Install the top plate.

Once the framing is complete, attach the 1½ x ¼ inch top plate. Apply glue to the joining surfaces, then bend it into place and hold it temporarily with clamps. Finally, secure it with brad nails.

⑤

⑥

Finish Up the — TRAILER INTERIOR

When the framing is complete, it's time to close up the trailer, starting from the inside out. The interior lining is really important because it acts as a skin that locks all the roof rafters together and tightly secures them in place.

There are several material options to pursue for the interior skin. I selected a high-end option that increases the price tag and time investment of my build significantly. I purchased some beautiful boards of reclaimed old-growth redwood and cedar, and then resawed them into 3/16-inch-thick strips of paneling that run lengthwise from end to end.

You can swap that out with a less difficult and expensive options like fiberboard paneling or 1/8-inch-thick finished plywood. The key is that you find a material that will bend to the curve of the trailer without breaking. It also needs to be durable to hold up to the weather, your dog that will want to sleep inside, and the dirty reality of roughing it in the woods.

7.1
Milling lumber

Milling the lumber is not easy and adds significant expense and/or time commitment to your trailer build. If you're trying to get through this thing quickly, you might modify this step with a much easier solution using any of a variety of bendable sheet goods.

My choice involved a labor-intensive woodworking process to mill 2-inch-thick rough lumber into a stack of ³⁄₁₆-inch-thick panels. This is an advanced woodworking process that requires a jointer, planer, and bandsaw. I happened to have access to those machines at my local makerspace, and spent nearly a dozen hours there sawing and flattening the material for the inside and outside of the trailer. The effort pays off though, thanks to the amazing colors and woodgrain that I'll get to admire for decades of camping trips to come. For me, the added commitment was worth it.

Note that if you choose to mill lumber to line your interior and exterior, you will need to select a joinery method before you mill. I tried a few options: beveled butt joints, square butt joints, and shiplap joinery. I also tried gluing the boards edge to edge and letting them float freely. Each method has its pros and cons, but I have found that techniques with glued edges, like edge to edge and glued shiplap, hold up to the elements best.

Choose a weather-resistant softwood. Wood selection is important, as you need a material that is strong and flexible when cut down to boards that are ³⁄₁₆-inch thick. Alaskan yellow cedar, redwood, and Western red cedar (left to right) work great. Look for dealers that serve boatbuilders and custom furniture makers.

SELECT A JOINERY STYLE.

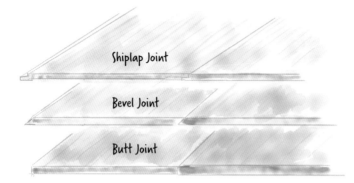

Shiplap Joint

Bevel Joint

Butt Joint

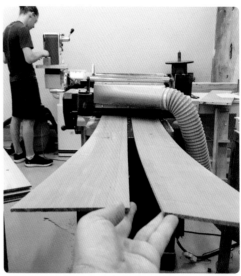

Resaw on the bandsaw.

Mill to thickness on the jointer/planer.

If using shiplap joinery, cut a rabbet on the tablesaw.

One down, many to go!

7.2
Lining the interior

Initially, I had imagined installing all the interior strips at the same time. My idea was to bend them into place by hand, coat the joining surfaces with exterior wood glue, then tack them in place with a brad nailer. However, the interior bend put too much pressure on the nails; they could not hold the boards in place for the glue to dry.

I scraped that idea and came up with a different approach. One by one, I installed each board by clamping it in place at each rafter with a layer of wood glue and letting it dry for 8 hours. This significantly slowed down the process and made me question the material choice vs. the effort to install it. An alternative like fiberboard would go in in just a few hours. Between work and family responsibilities, I managed to glue up one to two boards per day and got faster as the week progressed. By day seven, the interior was finished and ready to sand.

Note on joinery: The photos show a 45° beveled edge on each board. The idea was that each new board would hold down the adjacent one with a slight overlap at the edge joint. I applied glue to the joining beveled edges to lock them in place. This worked well, but you could also cut a rabbet into each edge to produce a shiplapped joint to ensure that there are no gaps between the panels.

1. Secure the boards.
The price of a paneled interior is a tedious installation process. Because each board requires so many clamps for a tight fit, it's best to install one at a time. Keep the boards a bit long on the kitchen side. You can trim that later on.

2. Don't skimp on glue.
Brush a layer of glue on each joining face to ensure a strong bond between the panels and rafters. Apply glue to the joining beveled edges.

3. Plan a strategy for a tight fit.
Set the panel in place, checking the fit at each end, and apply pressure at the center while you reach for a clamp.

4. Tighten your clamps.
The order in which you tighten the clamps matters. Start in the center and work your way out, closing the gap with each rafter. Use a waste block with each clamp to prevent marring the panels.

5. Check the overhead view.

Don't worry about messy glue lines on the outside. This all gets covered with insulation in the next chapter. But it's good practice for the exterior siding, where clean glue lines count.

6. Work your way across.

Continue attaching each board to the roof rafters one by one.

7. Cut away the excess around the vent hole.

Depending on the width of your panels, you may need to install a full-length board over any openings for windows and vents. Then cut away a section, like this area near the roof vent hole.

8. Trim the ends.
No need to perfectly align the panels at the kitchen galley side. It's easy to trim the ends flush with a handsaw once the glue has dried.

9. Finish it up.
This final panel will most likely turn out to be a custom width in order for it to fit tightly and account for any misalignment with the previous panels.

7.3
Upholstered headboard

The headboard offers additional space for storing personal items when camping or in tow. The space is easy to access whether you're opening the door to grab a flashlight, or thirsty water in the middle of the night. Adding an upholstered face to the cabinet doors also creates a comfy resting spot to read a book or watch a movie on your tablet.

I purchased all the supplies at a local fabric store. I started by cutting the foam slightly under the final desired dimensions. Then I measured and cut the materials to wrap around to the back, leaving plenty of extra material.

1. Lay down the upholstery material and cut to size.

2. Add a layer of muslin next.

3. Place the 1 ½-inch-thick cushion foam.

4. Place the ¼-inch-thick plywood backerboard.

5. Pull the material tight and staple the ends in place.

6. Trim the material for tight corners, cutting out a notch to remove the extra bulk.

7. Staple the final edges tightly in place.

8. The finished cushion should be bouncy and tight.

9. Build the box on top, starting with the back piece. Make sure it is the same size as the upholstered piece.

10. Apply glue to the edge of the back piece.

11. Attach both side pieces with glue and a brad nailer.

12. Now attach the ends in the same way.

13. One down, five to go.
Attach the cushion to the box with hook-and-loop tape.

14. Trim the headboard mounts.
Cut and fit cedar trim to cover all the faces of the headboard.

15. Install the cushions.
Attach the cushions to the boxes with two hinges.

16. Test out the cushion headboard.
The headboard serves as a comfortable back rest and a durable door to access the storage behind it.

7.4
A flexible storage system

There's limited room inside the trailer so I decided to keep the inside cabinetry to a minimum. Just enough to store a few days of clothes, bedding, towels, camping gear, electronics, and personal items that don't belong in the kitchen galley. The flexible design makes it useful in a variety of situations while remaining unobtrusive to the already-compact interior.

Rather than locking myself into a design configuration, I decided to design a sturdy mounting system that was flexible enough to accommodate a variety of storage configurations—from simple hangers for your luggage and gear to a complex cabinetry system.

The crux of the system is an extruded aluminum T-track that is easy to install and accepts a variety of standard T-bolts and mounts. These systems are available from woodworking supply retailers and marketed as "jig-building supplies" because they're useful to make shop tool accessories like a tablesaw fence. I installed two lengths of aluminum T-track in the front and back of the trailer cabin. The front piece screws to the inside of the headboard cabinet. On the back, the T-track screws to the top edge of the kitchen pantry cabinet.

I moved on to the next step in the build before building the interior components. I wanted to consider my storage needs more thoroughly. But I did pause to sketch some ideas that I'll tackle later on if I decide I need more elaborate cabinetry.

4

1. Close up the pantry.
Close up the kitchen cabinets from the inside. A sheet of ¼-inch-thick plywood will do, and it goes on quickly with some glue and a brad nailer.

2. Add a matching veneer.
Cover the plywood with cedar panels to match the interior skin.

3. Install flexibility with T-tracks.
Install universal aluminum T-track across the back that fit standard T-bolts or hex bolts for a variety of storage needs.

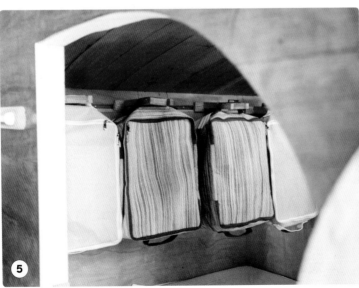

4. Create T-track accessories.
Start with a simple set of luggage hangers made from scrap mahogany left over from the trim. They are assembled with mortise-and-tenon joinery, glue, and screws.

5. Add a hanging luggage rack.
Four canvas luggage containers fit nicely against the cabin wall, providing storage for clothing.

Sketchbook:
IDEAS FOR INTERIOR CABINETRY

I figure it will take a few trips out on the road before I really understand the needs of the interior, so I decided to keep things simple to start but leave room for expansion later. Here are some sketches of my ideas for future interior storage systems that mount to the T-track.

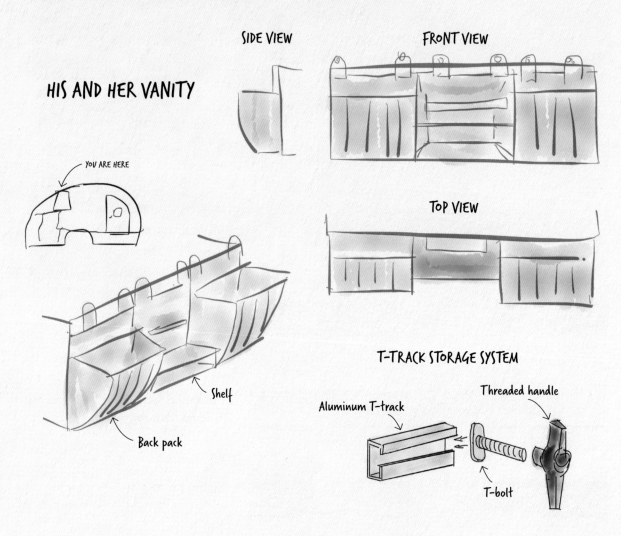

SIDE VIEW

FRONT VIEW

HIS AND HER VANITY

YOU ARE HERE

TOP VIEW

Shelf

Back pack

T-TRACK STORAGE SYSTEM

Threaded handle

Aluminum T-track

T-bolt

7.5
A bed platform with utility

At this point it became pretty clear that the inside floor framing below the bed offered valuable storage space. I had originally planned to insulate the box and close it up with ½-thick plywood, but scrapped that idea to make room for more storage. I installed hinged panels that made it easy to access camping supplies like fishing poles, collapsible tent chairs, and other random stuff.

There's limited space underneath the floor panels and I had to decide how much of it to take up with insulation vs. storage space. It was a trade off between temperature control and utility. I used material that resembled a yoga mat.

If you need the added insulation over storage space, cut strips of rigid foam insulation to fit snugly inside each section. This is also a good way to use up the scraps of ½-inch plywood used for the interior walls.

1. Install a foam liner.
To cover the exposed bare wood, lay down a wide sheet of thin foam, similar to a yoga mat. Look in the flooring section at the local big box home store. It's easy to attach the material with a staple gun.

2. A hinged hatch adds storage.
Make good use of the under-bed storage space with a collection of hinged hatch doors, two at the foot of the bed and one at the front on each side.

3. Place the hinged doors.
Position the doors in place before you attach the hinge sections to ensure that all the parts fit tightly.

4. Piano hinges and handles.
A piano hinge is easy to install and is a sturdy choice for this application. Pick up a matching handle in the same aisle at the hardware store.

5. Install a handle.
A flat folding handle is the best choice: it's easy to lift the door but doesn't interfere with the mattress on top.

7.6
Insulation

There's a bit of debate in the teardrop trailer world about this next step: is insulation actually required?

My instinct told me to pack all the framed walls with as much insulation as I could fit to help keep the trailer cooler in the summer and warmer in the winter. I can just imagine myself coming back from a long hike in the woods and flopping into the trailer for a quick afternoon nap. An insulated trailer will maintain a better temperature than a non-insulated one.

However, some trailer makers will tell you insulation is an exercise in futility. That's because there will rarely be a time when you find yourself closed up inside the trailer to take advantage of the insulated space.

A sealed-up trailer doesn't hold enough oxygen for people to breathe for a long period of time (yes, you read that correctly). When sleeping or hanging out in your trailer you'll need to keep a vent, window, or door open at all times to let in fresh air. This will result in the loss of insulated air.

Debate aside, since my walls were framed, I decided insulation was the best option. Sorting through the materials at the big box store, I landed on 1½-inch-thick rigid foam insulation. It's readily available in 4 x 8-foot sheets in a range of thicknesses, and provides reasonable R-value. It's also easy to cut with only a straightedge and utility knife and not very messy.

The insulation often comes with one white side and one foil side. Position it foil-side out to reflect outside heat away from the trailer interior. It's the right decision for us West Coast dwellers, where the climate is warmer and the goal is to keep the trailer cool. If you live in a cold-weather climate, consider flipping the insulation foil-side in to keep the heat inside the trailer cabin.

There's a lot written on how to properly insulate a structure. There are experts on the subject; I'm not one of them. So, I'd encourage you to do some research on this subject to choose your own way forward. Here's how I chose to proceed.

1. Fill the gaps.

Cut sheets of rigid foam insulation and fit them to each cavity between the framing. The foam should fit tightly without glue. Don't leave gaps around the edges or air will get in.

2. Small cavities are easy to fill.

Use the actual dimensions of the opening to mark, measure, and cut foam scraps to size.

3. Ensure clean cuts.

For long cuts, lay the insulation on the ground and use a straightedge to guide your utility knife blade. First score the cut, then cut deep. Snap it, then cut the final face.

4. Fill the roof.

Just like the sides, fill the roof cavities with insulation to keep the excess heat and cold out.

5. Dust off the trailer.

While rigid foam insulation is the least messy option of the bunch, it still creates a bunch of foam dust. Just roll your trailer outside and sweep it off after the insulation is installed.

— *Frame the* —
DOORS AND WINDOW HATCH

Keep the water out: that's the mantra you'll want to repeat when building your teardrop trailer, especially when constructing the windows, hatches, and doors. Think like a raindrop. Where would you go if you landed right here? Or there? Now add gusty winds and a traveling speed and you'll believe me when I advise you to *weatherproof everything*.

The simplest method to install doors and windows that don't leak is to buy the commercial variety, which are available for a reasonable price. They're relatively easy to install and come with all the flashing and seals that ensure a dry fit.

I decided to take the more complicated route and design custom doors and windows from scratch. On the upside, I produced a curve that matched the curve of the trailer roofline and was two-toned like the rest of the trailer. On the downside, I was forced to solve the waterproofing challenge on my own, without an off-the-shelf flashing product. As you read through this section, think critically about the level of investment it takes to go this direction, versus buying commercial doors and moving on. In the end, like every design decision, it's a calculation of time and effort.

WATERPROOF THRESHOLDS

Getting the doors and windows to fit requires a lot of sketching. Mine didn't end up exactly as drawn, but this is the kind of fit I aimed to achieve.

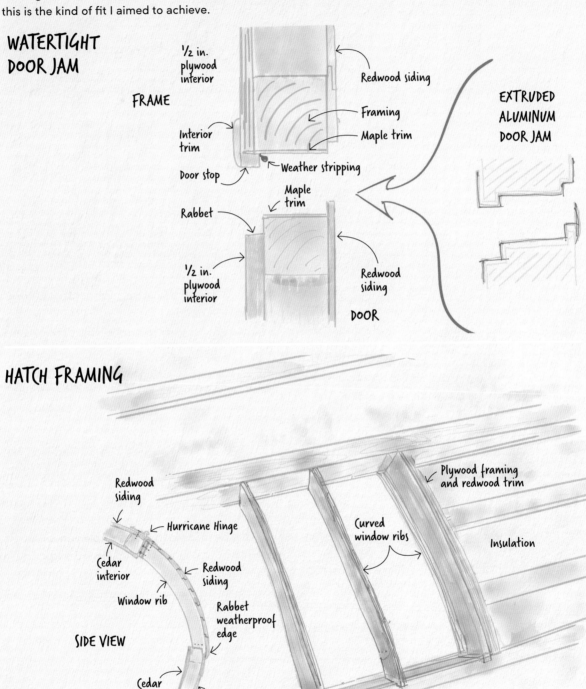

WATERTIGHT DOOR JAM

½ in. plywood interior

Redwood siding

FRAME

Framing

Maple trim

Interior trim

Weather stripping

Door stop

Maple trim

Rabbet

½ in. plywood interior

Redwood siding

DOOR

EXTRUDED ALUMINUM DOOR JAM

HATCH FRAMING

Redwood siding

Hurricane Hinge

Plywood framing and redwood trim

Cedar interior

Redwood siding

Curved window ribs

Window rib

Insulation

Rabbet weatherproof edge

SIDE VIEW

Cedar interior

Redwood siding

8.1
Trim the doorframe

At this point, the doorframe is not ready yet to accept a door. While the interior plywood wall is cut to the shape of the opening, the framing around it is not. There are sections where there is no 2 x 2 material, only insulation.

To ensure a good door fit, create an interior doorframe that is straight, square, and true to the door opening. The material I use to make laminated skateboard decks—⅛-inch-thick maple—is a perfect choice to create the bend around the door curve and produce a durable frame.

1. Glue on each strip.
Cut a bunch of strips from sheets of ⅛-inch-thick maple veneer, or mill your own thin wood strips.

2. Tape them in place.
Apply glue to the veneer and clamp it down with tape. It takes a lot, so buy a few rolls to complete the job.

8.2
Build the doors to fit

Once you have a finished opening, turn your attention to building the doors to fit. Remember way back when you cut out the doors from the plywood sides? I hope you kept them, because those cutouts serve as the foundation for each door.

The first step is to trim the edges of the door straight and square so the piece fits in the new door opening with about ¼-inch clearance on all sides. Once cut to size, glue and screw framing to the edges of the door and trim off the waste that hangs over. Finally, apply the same trim material you used for the door framing to the outside edge of the door.

By now, you should have about ⅛-inch clearance around the entire door. This space will allow for the installation of weather stripping so that the door to fits inside snuggly but without jamming.

In this step of the project you'll only complete the doors halfway. The final steps take place later after the exterior siding has been applied. Put them aside for now.

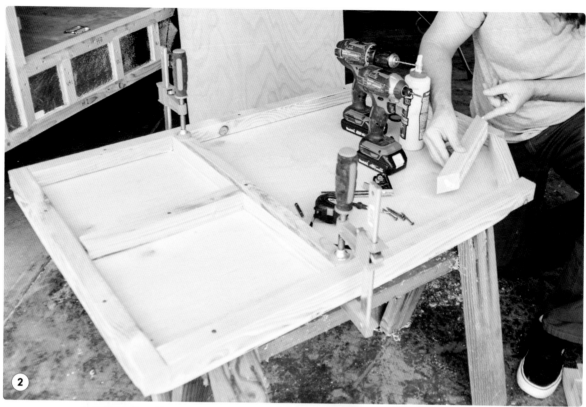

1. Save the scraps.
Remember when you cut out the door from the side panel way back in this project? They become the starting point for each door.

2. Frame the edges.
Cut 2 x 2 pine parts to wrap around the frame of the entire door.

3. Attach the framing.
Like the trailer framing, attach each piece with glue, then clamp them while you drive in wood screws to secure the parts.

4

5

4. Cut the excess.
Use a jigsaw to cut away the excess framing material that extends past the edge of the door. Cut close to the line but don't cross it!

5. Make the edges square.
A handplane or Surform rasp helps square up the door edge. Check your work with a carpenter's square.

6. Wrap the door edges.
Use ⅛-inch-thick maple veneer to wrap the edges of the doors. Glue them down and hold them in place with tape.

7. Rounding the corners.
Wet the thin maple down with glue and let that soak it, and it will easily bend without breaking around the curved corner.

8.3
The front hatch

When you're lying in bed looking up, tired and satisfied from a happy day of camping, you'll be glad you installed a front window hatch to provide a wide-screen view of the sky above.

To keep things easy, I designed this as a hatch, not a window, so there was no need to mess around with curved glass. The main challenge was to design around the Hurricane Hinge and some type of window trim and flashing system that would move water away from the trailer interior.

The window sits proud of the trailer surface by ¼ inch and hangs over by the same distance on the bottom edge, creating a raised edge of flashing. The rest of the waterproofing work comes later when I install the exterior siding.

1. Create curved hatch parts.
The hatch is made from a series of curved ribs cut from ¾-inch plywood to match the shape of the trailer profile. The ribs sit proud of the window opening by ¼ inch and hang over the edge at the bottom to prevent water intrusion at the bottom.

2. Finish the window openings.
Glue a curved piece on the left and right side of the window hatch to create a smooth flat surface for the window to close against.

3. Assemble the hatch.
Glue and nail the ribs to a top and bottom plate. Most of the strength comes later on when the exterior boards are attached.

4. Check the fit.
Set the window hatch in place and see how it fits! Make any fine-tune adjustments with a sander or handplane.

9.1
Run the wiring

A collection of electrical fixtures inside and outside the trailer are powered by a deep-cycle marine battery installed in the kitchen galley. The system includes two cabin reading lights, two exterior lights, a kitchen light, an electric fan, and two cigarette lighters where you can plug in up to four USB chargers to power up small devices like a cell phone or Bluetooth speaker.

Unlike the trailer wiring, which came partially installed, the cabin electrical system is built from scratch and designed from the ground up. This means not only do you have to learn the technical skills of installing an electrical wiring system, you also must understand the theory of it all in order to design a wiring configuration that is safe and efficient.

I started with the positive lines, running one black wire for each fixture from the battery box to the location where the fixture will be installed. Leave some extra slack in case you need to adjust anything later on. The light switches each require a short run of wire to bring power from the switch to the fixture. Tape the wires down as you go.

Next, lay out the negative ground wires. These don't need to feed all the way back to the battery box. Instead, I identified a few points around the steel trailer frame to attach the ground wires. Because the battery is grounded to the trailer frame, each of the fixtures can ground to it as well to complete the current.

Once everything is laid out, cut out channels and drill holes in the framing to make room for the wires. Then start connecting the wires and plugging things in!

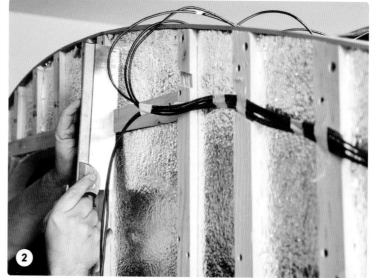

1. Dry-fit the wires.

Take a look at the illustration on page 130 and do a rough layout of the wiring. Run the wires where you think you'll need them and tape them into place to get a sense of what you're dealing with.

2. Cut a channel with a handsaw.

Once the arrangement is set, cut a channel in the framing anywhere the wires need to cross. Use a handsaw to quickly cut the two sides of the channel; it doesn't need to be perfect.

3. Clean it out with a chisel.

Remove the channel waste with a chisel to make room for the bundle of wires. It should be deep enough that the wires sit flush in the framing without interfering with the exterior siding.

4. Run the wires neatly.
Set the wires neatly in the channels and tape them in place to stay put before the walls go in and lock everything in place.

5. Feed the wire in tight quarters.
Rather than cutting a channel at the top edge, where the gluing surface is critical, drill a few holes to feed the wire through.

6. Bundle and label the wires.
Run all the positive wires to the kitchen galley to meet up with the circuit breaker box and battery. The ground wires are distributed to connection points around the trailer frame.

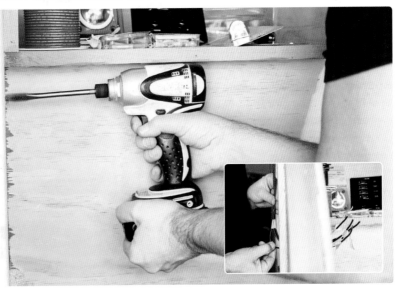

1
2
3

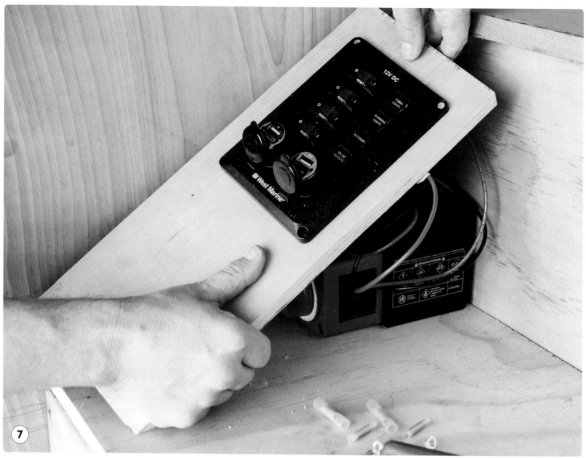

7. Install the circuit breaker.
Temporarily mount the circuit breaker in the kitchen galley in the general location where it will be installed later on. Leave some slack in your wires so you can move it around for final fitting.

8. Check your connections.
The fixtures are distributed across four circuits. Those connect to a main power switch, and finally connect to the battery. Buy a compact 12-volt battery to test your connections.

9.2
Install the fixtures

For each of the fixtures and switches, you'll need to determine the right time to install based on the location. Anything that attaches to the outside of the trailer will have to wait until the exterior siding goes on. For now, just feed the wires to the location with some extra slack and make sure the power works. The inside fixtures can go in immediately if you don't mind covering or temporarily removing them when it comes time to apply a wood finish.

Installing the two interior lights and the four switches involves cutting into the walls and insulation. I did this work with a drill bit to create a pilot hole for my jigsaw blade. The downside to this fast and dirty approach is that I created some tearout at the edges that required a creative cover-up. A more sophisticated approach would be to create a simple template and cut out the openings with a flush-trim router bit. Cut these in chapter 5.4 if you're confident in your plans.

1. Add interior LED lights.
Small LED lights mount easily to the interior wall. One on each side provides his-and-her reading lights and easy access at night.

2. Install on/off switches.
LED switches operate the interior and exterior lights on each side.

3. Create a simple switch plate.

Cut out a basic switch plate from a sheet of maple veneer to cover up the tearout around the edge of the two cutouts for the switches.

4. Wire the switches.

Attach the ends of each wire from the battery, the two light fixtures, and ground connections.

5. Connect the wires.

Join the wires with connectors. Strip the insulation from a bit of the end of the wire, then cinch down each side in the connector to ensure the wires stay joined.

6. Wire the ceiling fan.
The ceiling fan gets its own circuit. You've already run a positive line from the circuit breaker and a negative line down to the trailer frame. Now connect the fan wiring to the wires from the breaker.

7. Check the ground wires.
Feed a ground wire to each electrical fixture from the metal trailer frame.

8. Connect to the steel frame.
Attach the ground wires with a ring connector. Various sections of the electrical system should be grounded at multiple points of the steel trailer frame.

9.3
Factory-installed trailer lights

The trailer electrical configuration is a standard 7-pin plug that runs off the car battery to power the driving lights, the electric trailer brakes, and charge up the auxiliary battery to run the trailer's on-board 12-volt electrical system.

I chose to have the wiring and circuit box installed by the factory dealer. That included securing the ground wire to the trailer frame and also connecting the brake line for the proportional brakes. But I left the other five wires dangling so that I could install the fixtures for the running lights, blinkers, and brake lights after the trailer siding went on.

A trailer this size requires a handful of travel lights to ensure visibility and safety on the road. On each side there are orange front running lights, and red running lights at the tail end. The bumper has a left and right blinker and brake light, as well as a

center lamp above the license plate. Additional running lights installed on the fender or top edge would provide added safety and may be required in some states depending on your trailer size.

Finishing these off was relatively easy since the wiring was already installed. I just needed to decide where to mount the lights and make sure there was appropriate blocking in place to catch the screws. I also had to run the additional wiring for the ground and extend the running lights' power to multiple fixtures.

If your vehicle is not already wired to tow a trailer, you'll need to outfit it with aftermarket parts. I had the tow-hitch and wiring installed by a professional installer because this requires tapping into your vehicle's electronics, which was out of my comfort zone.

1. Wire the rear runner lights.

Drill a hole to feed the wire for the rear running light; run the wires through. Install a ground wire and an additional positive wire to bring power back to the light fixture above the license plate.

2. Wire the blinkers and brake lights.

A positive line feeds the rear blinkers and brake light. Most trailer electrical systems follow a standard color coding to identify each light. You can run into systems with different color coding, so be sure to take good notes you can reference as needed, especially once the walls are closed up.

1
2
3

3. Ground the tail lights.
Feed a ground wire from each of the fixtures to various points around the trailer frame.

4. Fast-forward to the fixtures.
After the exterior siding goes on, you can install the fixtures. Here's a look ahead at that process. These waterproof connectors shrink to fit when heated up quickly with a lighter.

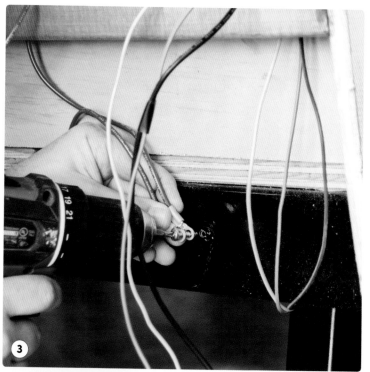

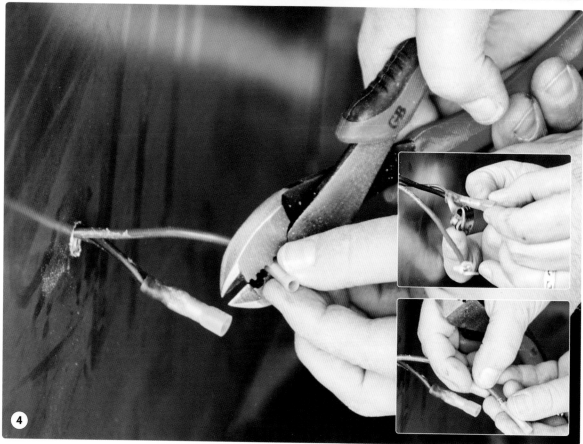

UPGRADE WITH A SOLAR CHARGING SYSTEM

When you run an on-board battery at the campsite, eventually you'll end up with a run-down battery. It could be faster than you think, depending how many watts you're drawing. My system is designed to recharge when the car is running. Power is delivered from the car battery to the trailer battery— as long as the car battery is at a minimum charge to prevent your car from running out of juice.

I didn't immediately pursue solar on my trailer build. But I called up an old friend who pursued a career in solar energy to understand my options.

The most common option is a 75 to 100W (watt) photovoltaic panel and a 100AH (amp hour) battery with an appropriately sized charge controller and inverter. There are multiple kits available on the Internet that package these up.

At the high end, I looked at one complete solar kit marketed to 12-volt RVs and boat owners looking to get off the grid. It puts out 1500W power and comes with an inverter box, a solar panel, solar cable and MC4 connectors, and a controller. Someday, I'll consider installing a set.

This solar panel kit for powering 12-volt systems is a great addition. Shown is WindyNation 100 Watt Solar Panel Kit with 1500W VertaMax Power Inverter, B00HK0YOPU.

(10)

— Install the —
EXTERIOR SIDING AND ROOF

When it comes to installing the exterior wrap of materials on your teardrop trailer, once again, think like a raindrop. Even better: think like a raindrop making impact at 60 miles an hour driving down the road while the wind is blowing sideways in freezing temperatures. (Okay, maybe you'll want to pull over under those conditions.) On the flip side, it must also be able to stand up to hot temperatures and direct sun.

My point is that your trailer must stand up to the most brutal wet conditions; more than any stationary home. Tight joinery and strong sealed seams are critical to success at this step of the process.

The most common material to use for the exterior is sheet aluminum against plywood sheathing, which protects against the weather, requires minimal finish, and looks cool. But aluminum is not your only option. I chose an unconventional two-tone finish with aluminum on the bottom and wood paneling on top.

A BETTER WAY TO INSTALL SIDING

Coming up with a method to install the exterior siding so it's totally waterproof took some sketching and brainstorming. My first concern was creating water-tight joints at the corners and the seam where the redwood side panels meet up with the aluminum. My second concern was how to physically attach the long roof panels from end to end. Below are some ideas and concepts that got me thinking.

WATERTIGHT SEAMS

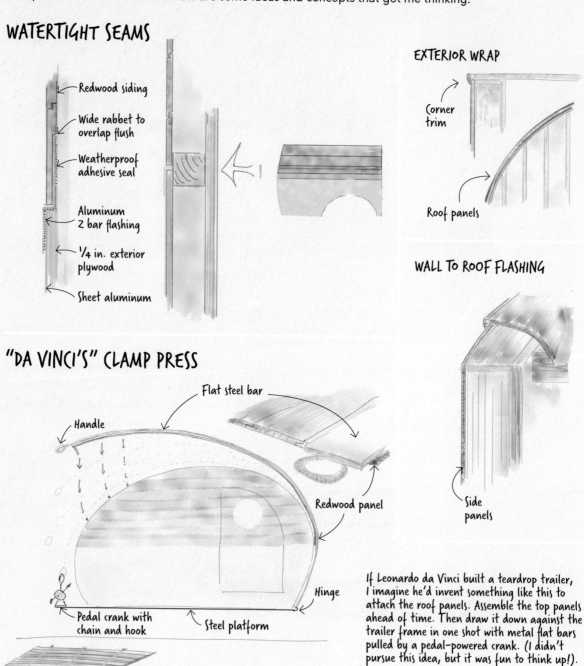

Redwood siding

Wide rabbet to overlap flush

Weatherproof adhesive seal

Aluminum Z bar flashing

¼ in. exterior plywood

Sheet aluminum

EXTERIOR WRAP

Corner trim

Roof panels

WALL TO ROOF FLASHING

Side panels

"DA VINCI'S" CLAMP PRESS

Flat steel bar

Handle

Redwood panel

Hinge

Pedal crank with chain and hook

Steel platform

If Leonardo da Vinci built a teardrop trailer, I imagine he'd invent something like this to attach the roof panels. Assemble the top panels ahead of time. Then draw it down against the trailer frame in one shot with metal flat bars pulled by a pedal-powered crank. (I didn't pursue this idea, but it was fun to think up!).

10.1
Plywood underneath

The aluminum half of the trailer requires the installation of ¼-inch-thick plywood sheathing. This adds some extra rigidity to the trailer walls and creates a flat solid surface for the aluminum to prevent it from getting easily dinged and dented.

Because the fenders were pre-installed on my trailer, I had to cut a half-circle into the plywood and the aluminum to fit. This is not ideal, because it creates a danger spot where water could get in and damage the wood. In this situation, create a bent laminated template that matches the curve of the fender. and use it to mark and cut the side panels to fit.

1. Bend a template for the fender.
Cut four wood strips from any bendy material you can find—I used some ⅛-inch-thick maple skateboard veneer. Apply glue to all the joining sides.

2. Clamp it to the fender.
Clamp the laminated parts to the fender and let the glue dry for at least 3 hours to ensure the bend maintains its shape when the clamps are removed.

3. Check your final fit.
When the glue dries, remove the clamps and confirm that the template retained the correct bend and is ready to use.

4. Trace out the template.
Use the bent-laminated curve to draw a line on the exterior plywood where it will straddle the fender.

5. Cut to the line.
Cut out the fender with a jigsaw, making sure not to cross over the line.

6. Dry-fit for fine tuning.
Clamp the panel in place to check your fit and mark the remaining cuts.

7. Mark the curve.
Mark the front and back end of the panel to finish cutting it to shape and size.

8. Cut to fit.
Cut to just outside the marked line with a jigsaw.

9. Trim the edge flush.
With each piece positioned exactly where you want it, trim the edges flush with a hand-held router and a bearing-guided, flush-trim router bit.

10. Mark the position.
Mark a few spots around the edges so that you can easily remove and line up the plywood panel in the exact spot.

10.2
Fitting the aluminum siding

The thin-gauge 0.032-inch-thick aluminum I selected can be cut and shaped with the same tools used to cut plywood. A jigsaw makes the rough cuts, and the edges get cleaned up with a bearing-guided flush trim bit. Just be careful when dealing with the aluminum dust. Wear extra safety gear and keep the dust contained for easy cleanup. Getting aluminum dust in your eye is a guaranteed trip to urgent care.

There are a few things to keep in mind while working with this material. First, the thin aluminum is easy to bend, especially at the corners and edges. For example, if the jigsaw blade gets caught on the edge during cutting, it can pull the material and create an unwanted bend. To prevent that, always make sure to have a sacrificial board underneath the aluminum so that the blade cuts through both the wood and the aluminum. Another option is to sandwich the aluminum between two sheets of plywood when cutting. This will help prevent bending, and provides a solid, sturdy cutting surface.

Second, aluminum scratches easily. Despite taking great care to lay the material down on a flat smooth surface when cutting, and storing it safely, a few of my pieces sustained some minor scratches during the prepping process. There may be ways to buff out the scratches, but it made me realize that keeping my finished trailer scratch-free was going to be challenging.

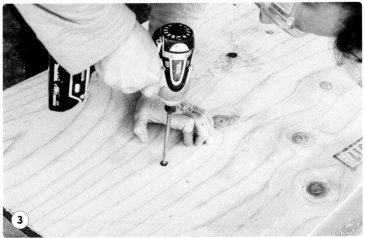

1. Cut the aluminum with a jigsaw.
Lay the material good side down on a smooth clean surface to prevent scratching. Then lay the plywood panel from the previous steps on top to use as a template and cutting guide.

2. Keep it clamped.
Continually reset your clamps so that your jigsaw blade is always cutting within a few inches of one. This prevents the aluminum from bouncing around during the cut.

3. Drill holes for wiring.
When the aluminum sheet is cut to size, use your plywood panel to locate and cut the hole for the electrical wiring.

4. Check your fit.
Temporarily mount the plywood panels and aluminum back onto the trailer to check your fit. Use the marked guidelines to position the pieces exactly as planned.

ALTERNATIVES TO UNFINISHED ALUMINUM

Unfinished aluminum requires surface prep and a finish to protect it from the elements. Without a finish, unfinished aluminum catches every fingerprint, shows drips and streaks from oxidization in wet weather, and scratches easily. If you're interested in skipping the extra work to finish the surface yourself, take a look at one of these alternative products.

Painted Aluminum Sheet and Coil

Polyester painted aluminum sheet and coil is a thin, colored aluminum material used as an exterior material in a variety of industry applications, including outdoor signs and advertising, building and architecture, and transportation. A version of the material with an acrylic paint finish is used to make large box car trailers for long-haul trucking.

Polyester painted aluminum sheets can be found in a few dozen stock paint colors, and can be customized to suit, which makes it great for matching your trailer to your tow vehicle's color. It comes in a variety of sizes, from thin rolls (.008 millimeter) to thick .080-millimeter sheets, and in standard widths up to 60 inches wide. Some dealers will be able to cut it for you to custom dimensions using a collection of industrial tooling—slitting, blanking, and shearing—which leaves perfect edges you won't get at home with DIY cutting tools.

Anodized Aluminum

If you like the natural finish of raw aluminum, a more durable option is anodized aluminum. Anodizing is an electrochemical process that converts the metal surface into an anodic oxide finish. It is corrosion and abrasion resistant and does not fade, chip, peel, or flake. It is also fingerprint resistant.

The anodizing process does change the surface color; it is available in clear, bronze, gold, and copper anodized. Finishes include satin, bright, and brushed. It's also an ideal base for adhesion of paints, inks, substrates, and vinyl film.

Fiberglass Filon

Fiberglass Filon siding is another popular choice for the exterior of a trailer or RV. The light and durable material is constructed of plastic fibers woven together and reinforced with glass fiber, allowing it to bend to a form and hold its shape. Fiberglass Filon is available on the Internet in custom-sized rolls big enough to cover most trailer walls in width and height. It measures .045 millimeters in thickness, or about 1/16 inch.

Foam Core Aluminum Composite Panels

About an hour north of Atlanta, in the hills of Georgia, you'll probably find Nick Orlando in his garage workshop making something or fixing something else. By trade he does work painting, home remodeling, and basic carpentry in the small county where he grew up. Nick took a unique approach to his trailer build. His teardrop is about 90% aluminum, assembled using SPAX screws, polyurethane construction adhesive, and an adhesive tape called VHB from 3M. The sides are made from a .32-millimeter-thick aluminum composite material laminated to a polyethylene core. The material comes in dimensional panels like plywood and is strong and rigid for its weight. In fact, it weighs less than a piece of ⅛-inch-thick

This teardrop trailer is built almost entirely from aluminum to minimize potential moisture damage.

plywood of the same dimensions, Nick notes. "Less wood means less rot. A lot of campers from the '80s get a roof leak and before you know, it your walls are full of mold."

10.3

Install the exterior wood siding

Things really start to come together as you begin applying the plywood to the bottom and the redwood siding to the top portion of the trailer walls.

I debated a lot about how to deal with wood movement here. Ultimately I decided to glue the panels in place edge to edge. This technique has held up to the weather really well.

To ensure there were no gaps in the seams, exterior wood glue is a good choice for adhering the panels to the wall. It will provide a strong hold for years to come and has some flexibility to absorb torque and twist in the walls when going over bumps and dips in the road.

Aligning the grain is also an important detail to keep in mind. Before you start attaching the panels, lay them down and check to make sure grain and color match from one panel to the next.

①

1. Apply wood glue.
Spread glue on all the surface faces that will make contact with your bottom plywood pieces. Look out for drips.

2. Nail in place.
Hold the plywood panels in place temporarily with a clamp, then secure with brad nails.

3. Mark and cut the redwood.
To ensure continuous grain on the sides, place the panel across the full length of the trailer and mark the cut for the door. Save these pieces, and mark the order, so the door grain matches perfectly.

4. Glue it up.
Apply glue to the joining surfaces, especially the edge of the redwood where it meets the plywood.

1
2
3
4
5
6

5. Secure with brad nails.
Tack the redwood panels in place one by one. Take care when nailing; you want to leave as little trace as possible.

6. Feed the wires.
Remember to feed the wires for the exterior light through the redwood panel before attaching it permanently.

7. Look out for wires.
Stay clear of your electrical wiring when driving nails. At this precarious point, make sure to move the wires out of the way. When in doubt, don't nail it.

8. Repeat on the other side.
Install the siding one by one, gluing and nailing in place.

9. Flush-trim to a finish.
After the glue dries, use the flush-trim router bit to cut the overhang from the door and the outer edges.

10.4

Install the redwood roof panels

In the photography for the roof panels, you will see the shiplap joints. As the name suggests, this technique was born out of boat building, where the wood is exposed to extreme moisture and requires space to shrink and expand comfortably.

I used this joint for a different reason. I glued ship-lapped joinery to prevent the panels from moving around and cracking the epoxy finish that is applied later on. However, the overlapping joint allowed me to be less fussy when it came to lining up the boards edge to edge across the long span of the joint. If a small gap appeared, it was okay because they overlapped enough to close the joint adequately.

1. Use marine adhesives.
Marine adhesive is the material of choice for shiplapped joints. It flexes but sticks under extreme conditions. My recommendation is 3M Marine Adhesive Sealant Fast Cure 5200.

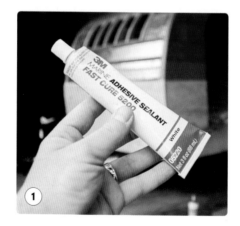

2. Install the front panel.
Set the plywood panel in place and secure it with brad nails. A clamp helps keep stubborn areas in check.

3. Apply a bead of glue.
Run a bead of marine adhesive just shy of the edge and on the crossbeams—enough for the first redwood panel. Wear disposable gloves to keep your skin glue-free.

4. Toenail it.
Drive the nails at an angle so they act as clamps while the glue dries. Use actual clamps to secure the panel while nailing.

1

2

3

4

5

6

5. Move on down the line.
Continue on to the next strip, gluing and nailing as you go.

6. Keep track of cutoffs.
Come up with a system to keep track of the cutoff order. This way you can used the offcuts on the hatch and keep the grain continuous.

7. Cover the openings.
Install the panels over all your window openings to keep the curve continuous. You'll cut those out after the glue dries.

8. Steady as you go.
Make sure you have a sturdy base to stand on when you attach the panels on the roof.

9. Nearing the end.
Continue the process until you reach the other side.

5

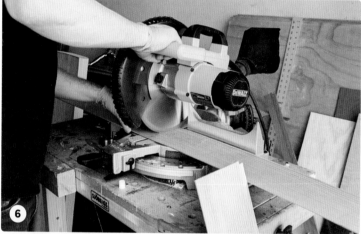

6

7

8

10. Reveal the window and vent.
Use the flush-trim router bit to cut away the window and vent openings that were covered by the redwood panels. These pieces will be discarded.

11. Reinforce the panels.
Be prepared when you remove the material at the window: it relieves a ton of stress in the wood from the bend. You may need to quickly add glue and clamp the edges to prevent them from popping off the trailer body frame.

10.5

Finish the doors and window hatch

Earlier in the book I assembled the doors to a partial stage and set them aside. Now it's time to bring them back out to install the window and exterior. The pause in construction gave me some time to research the best options in trailer windows. Going back to my thesis statement: my goal is to create a watertight structure even under the most torrential weather conditions.

The first place to look is with commercial trailer window manufacturers. Several window options are available online and through local RV dealers and repair shops. These offer high-quality flashing and seals, open and close easily, and sometimes include bug screens or tinted glass. Cut a hole to size based on a template provided with the window, and it installs quickly without much fuss.

I found one round window for sale on the Internet that appeared to fit the bill: a 12-inch non-opening porthole designed for a van. I ordered one for each door.

①

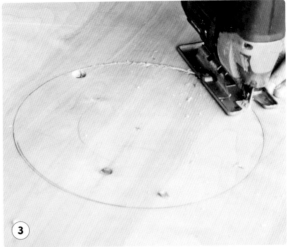

5

1. Use a jig for a perfect circle.
Craft together a circle template from scrap wood. Drive a screw through the jig and into your workpiece, then hold a pencil at the other end at a 6-inch radius.

2. Scribe the line.
Retrace the circle with a razor blade to scribe a line in the plywood. This creates a fresh cut line and prevents tearout when you cut it out with the jigsaw.

3. Cut out the circle.
Drill an entry hole on the inside of the circle near the edge. Cut carefully just inside the scribed line with a fine-toothed jigsaw blade. Steady as you go.

4. Make an octagonal frame.
Create a wood frame around the perimeter of the circular cutout from eight equally cut segments with 22.5° cuts. Adhere the frame to the door with wood glue.

5. Attach the frame.
Clamp the eight segments of the window frame to the plywood surface until the glue dries.

6. Install blocking for hinges.
Glue a block in the location where the door hinges will be installed to provide a solid footing for the hinge hardware. Use your hinge to determine the correct placement.

7. Gather the tools.
Use a combination of the jigsaw and bearing-guided flush-trim router bits to trim the window framing to a perfect circle.

8. Cut out the window frame.
Saw away the extra window frame material with the jigsaw, cutting closely to the edge of the circle without crossing into it.

9. Trim from the other side.
Match the circle with a pair of flush-trim bits from both sides of the door.

6

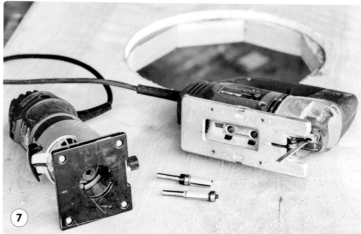

7

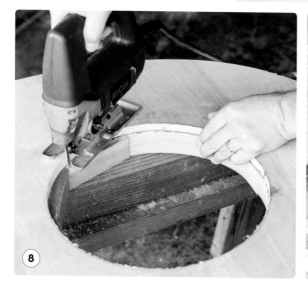

8

9

10. Test the fit.
Now check your fit to see how it nestles inside the door opening.

11. Install the plywood siding.
Glue and nail a piece of plywood to the lower half of the door to match the trailer side and trim flush with the router.

12. Finish with redwood siding.
Install the redwood siding in the same order it was saved to create a continuous grain pattern along the trailer side.

13. Trim away the waste.
Reveal the final door profile by trimming away the overhanging siding with a flush-trim bit.

14. Take a good look!
The door fits. If yours doesn't, adjust as needed.

15. Install the window parts.
The window is commercially available and includes a set of interlocking rings and a circular piece of tinted auto glass.

16. Finish the front hatch.
Install the redwood siding in a horizontal pattern on the front hatch with glue and clamps.

17. Add a slight bend.
Use a brad nailer to secure each board against the curve.

18. The final stretch.
Finish up with the final sections of exterior siding on the edge of the kitchen galley.

10.6

Attach the aluminum siding

While it may seem out of order, the last step to completing the siding is to attach the aluminum panels to the plywood walls. Contact cement is the adhesive of choice.

Unfortunately, it's also highly toxic and requires great care and attention to safety when using—especially in your garage.

①

1. Apply the adhesive.
Roll on contact cement with a paint roller and let dry for at least 10 minutes before joining the pieces.

2. Place the aluminum.
Once the aluminum touches the plywood, the contact cement will stick, so make sure you line it up properly.

3. Make hard contact.
Apply even pressure to the entire surface to ensure that the contact cement adheres properly.

4. Almost there!
This thing is really starting to look like a trailer!

— *Build the* —
KITCHEN HATCH

The kitchen galley is the pride of the teardrop trailer. It has a clean surface for food preparation, ample storage for provisions and supplies, and a workspace to accomplish all sorts of tasks at the campsite. Plus, it contains the hub of the on-board electrical system and offers a place to charge your cell phone and other electronics.

The galley is accessed with a large lifting hatch that hinges open at the top and stays ajar with a set of gas-shock props.

I decided to leave this step in the project toward the end for a few reasons. First, the hatch seemed like the most difficult piece to build. Not only is it a complex shape, but it also must be designed for heavy use, regularly opening and closing, all the while keeping its tight fit inside the hatch opening. It also is the primary defense to keep the water out of your kitchen galley. And if it can't keep it out, the hatch must redirect the water away from any trailer parts that aren't waterproof. Full disclosure: it took me two tries to build a sturdy hatch.

CONCEPTS FOR THE KITCHEN HATCH

It is a good idea to do lots of sketching on the rear hatch before you began cutting and assembling parts to make sure you anticipate possible failures and mishaps.

WORKING OUT THE REAR HATCH

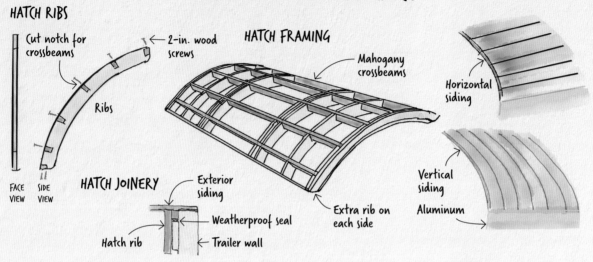

HATCH RIBS

Cut notch for crossbeams

← 2-in. wood screws

Ribs

FACE VIEW   SIDE VIEW

HATCH FRAMING

Mahogany crossbeams

Horizontal siding

Vertical siding

Aluminum

Extra rib on each side

HATCH JOINERY

Exterior siding

Weatherproof seal

Hatch rib

← Trailer wall

ATTACHING THE EXTERIOR PANELS

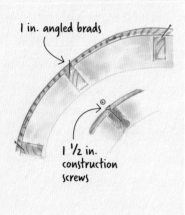

1 in. angled brads

1 ½ in. construction screws

A WATERTIGHT HATCH SEAL

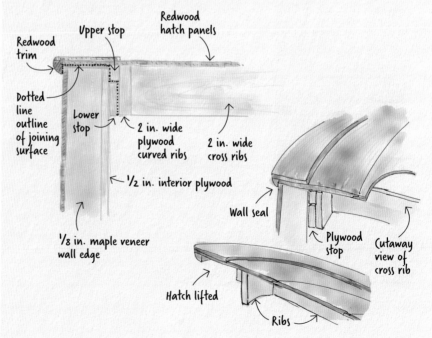

Redwood trim

Upper stop

Redwood hatch panels

Dotted line outline of joining surface

Lower stop

2 in. wide plywood curved ribs

2 in. wide cross ribs

½ in. interior plywood

⅛ in. maple veneer wall edge

Wall seal

Plywood stop

Cutaway view of cross rib

Hatch lifted

Ribs

11.1
Construct the hatch framing

The hatch is a series of curved ribs cut from a sheet of plywood and set flush with the curved walls. The ribs are connected by mahogany crossbeams that join with half-lap joints. This interlocking joinery keeps all the parts easily aligned during assembly and glue-up. When assembled, this creates a strong structure that is also flexible enough to absorb harsh bumps and bends on the road.

Because I set the top cabinetry too high in the trailer, I had to work around it when designing my hatch door. I first tried cutting a clearance notch into each rib, but that caused them to fail quickly. Ultimately, I ended up notching the cabinets. But if you heed my warning in chapter 5, you shouldn't have to deal with this hack.

1. Create a template for the ribs.
Clamp a piece of plywood to the trailer wall and use it as a guide to create a template with a matching curve. Mark the location of each crossbeam for reference.

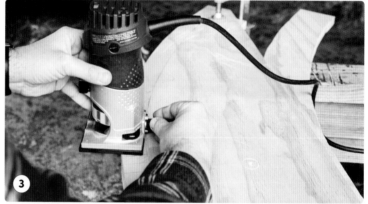

2. Rough-cut the ribs.
Use your template to cut out all the ribs. Cut them at least 1/16 inch oversized so you can clean them up to perfection with a router.

3. Shape each rib to fit.
Clamp each rough-cut rib to the template one at a time and cut to size with a bearing guided flush-trim router bit.

4. Cut the inside edge.
After establishing the outside edge of each rib, use a marking gauge to mark a line 2½ inches from the edge.

5. Cut a notch for the ribs.
If you set the cabinets too high in the kitchen, the hatch door won't close; if this happens, cut notches into the cabinetry for the ribs to fit when closed.

6. Dry-fit the ribs.
Set each of the ribs in place and confirm they align and sit flush with the trailer walls. Notice the outermost ribs are doubled up and have a notch that fits over the cabinetry.

7. Gang-cut the joinery.
Bundle up the rib parts to mark and cut the half-lap joinery. This ensures that all the parts will line up and assemble square.

1

2

8. Check the fit.
Dry-fit all the parts to check your joinery connections.

9. Mark the high points.
Identify any joints where the parts don't fit flush and clean those up with a chisel and file.

10. Assemble the frame.
Assemble the joinery in place using a dab of glue and a 1⅝-inch-long construction screw. Pilot drill to prevent splitting and to line up the joinery precisely.

11. Test-fit the hatch.
When assembled, the hatch framing should fit snuggly.

12. Install the bottom plate and edge stop.
Attach the edge plate across the bottom of the hatch. The outer curved parts provide additional strength and serve as a door stop. Cut these narrower than the others and glue them to the door frame.

11.2
Exterior paneling

The framework is mostly covered with exterior redwood panels that match the rest of the trailer. A small section has aluminum paneling to match the lower section of the trailer where it overlaps. The exterior paneling extends past both sides of the kitchen hatch wall to help create a waterproof seal when it is closed. Any water that does sneak through is redirected through a channel that leads down and out the tailgate just above the license plate.

You may be thinking about installing the redwood siding vertically to match the vertical grain direction of the roof panels and continue the grain. I tried this and it does not work. Glued shiplap joinery applied horizontally holds up well.

1. Prop the door open.
After holding the hatch in place with clamps, install the first row of exterior material with the door propped open so you can easily align the material and clamp it in place.

2. Install the panels.
Now start installing each panel one by one, using glue, screws, brads, and clamps. The bottom panel is plywood to match the level of the aluminum wrap.

3. Continue assembly.
Apply glue liberally on the joining surfaces, carefully align each board, then tack them in place with a brad nailer and screws at each rib.

4. Smooth the seams.
The shiplap joinery over the arch of the kitchen hatch can create some high points at the seams. Remove those with a no. 4 handplane (a palm-sander works too but creates more dust).

5. Trim the edges.
Clean up the edges of the kitchen hatch with a bearing-guided flush-trim router bit.

6. It's ready for install.
The hatch is ready for its hinge and final trim.

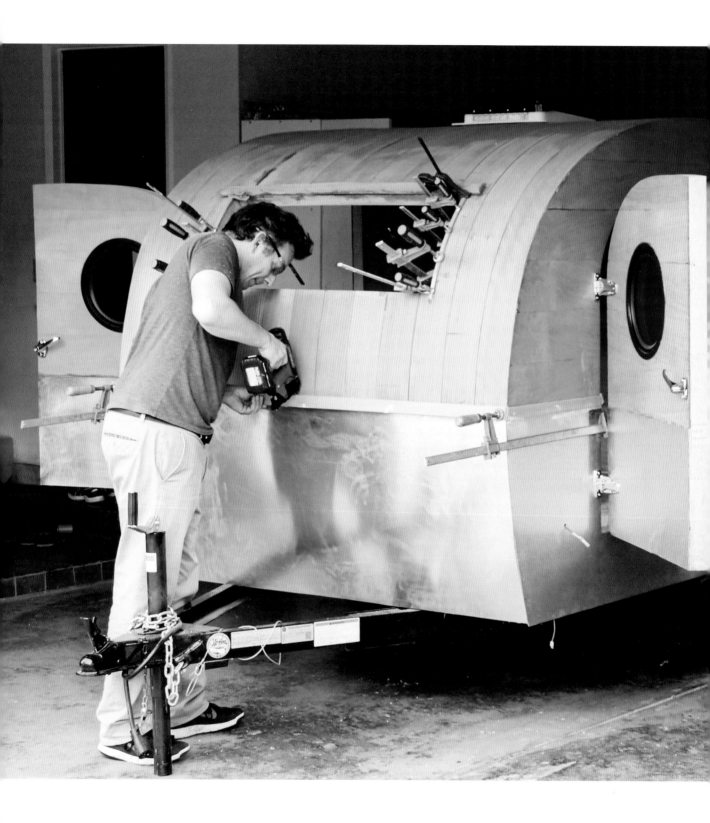

— *Install the* —
TRIM AND HARDWARE

Step back, take a deep breath, and take a good look at your trailer. By now, it's almost good enough to hitch up and drive off. But there are a few last things to button up, and they're important. Installing trim and weather stripping adds a fit-and-finish to your teardrop trailer that takes it to the next level.

Depending on the look and feel of your design, you have a few options when selecting materials for trim. In some cases, it's just a decorative element. In others, the trim serves as a vapor barrier, sealing seams and joints. Trim might also serve a protective purpose—either protecting you from bruises, or it from dings and scratches.

To match the materials of my trailer exterior, I chose to use a combination of extruded aluminum and mahogany.

The aluminum trim is applied in all corners to soften the edge and seal the open joints. Extruded aluminum is available in a variety of shapes and profiles and is easy to work with. It bends around curves, cuts with basic woodworking tools, and attaches simply with silicone adhesive and screws.

Mahogany wood trim is used throughout the trailer as a vapor barrier and as a threshold to join uneven surfaces.

12.1
Mahogany trim at the seams

Where the redwood paneling meets the sheet aluminum sides, I installed a simple mahogany threshold to protect the seam from water intrusion and join the uneven surfaces. I purchased lengths of mahogany at different widths at my local home center and shaped them with hand and power tools into simple trim profiles. Mahogany is a durable hardwood with similar coloring and weatherproof properties as redwood.

With the material milled to the proper width and thickness—just under ½-inch thick–I cut a rabbet into one edge with the trim router to create a notch where the material overlaps the aluminum. On the top edge, I added a slight bevel to prevent water from pooling up on the top edge of the trim. Instead, gravity does its job and sends the water streaming off the edge.

1. Prep the mahogany.
After milling the mahogany stock, cut a rabbet into the bottom inside corner and flatten the surfaces.

2. Fit the trim.
Install each section of trim one at a time, cutting each piece to fit. Use wood glue to adhere the top part of the trim to the redwood siding, and marine epoxy where it adheres to the aluminum siding.

3. Nail it in place.
Clamp the trim piece at each end and tack it in place with a brad nailer to hold it secure while the glue dries.

4. Create a seamless wrap.
The trim section on the door blends right into the rest of the trailer. Try to match the wood grain for even better-camouflaged seams.

12.2

A redwood bead

A raised bead of redwood trim outlines the entire outside edge of the trailer. This custom detail adds some nice visual appeal to the trailer lines. It also provides a bonus vapor barrier at the corner seam where wall meets roof.

I prepared a handful of long thin strips of redwood to just over ¼-inch square, ripped on the tablesaw from a single board. You might be thinking of increasing the dimensions for a more prominent edge trim, but ¼ inch is the max before the wood snaps when bending around the sharpest curves. Stack multiple strips for wider trim.

With the material prepped, it goes on pretty easy: apply glue to the joining surfaces and then tack it in place with a brad nailer. When the glue sets, shape it with a file and sandpaper.

1. Bend the strip and nail it.
A delicate strip of redwood is glued and nailed to the corner edge. Carefully bend as you go, securing it in place every few inches with a brad.

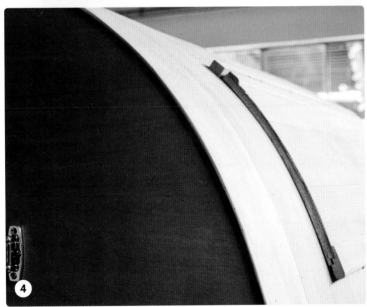

2. Match the curve.
Install a bead on the edge of the hatch. First lay tape underneath to guard against glue drips. While the hatch is closed, tack it with a brad nailer.

3. Round the bead.
Remove the marks from the brad nailer and round the sharp edges with a rasp, file, and sandpaper.

4. Ready for a finish.
The finished edge provides a nice shadow detail that really makes the curved lines pop.

12.3
Custom license plate and fixtures

The tailgate end of the trailer will probably get the most exposure to ogling on-lookers and long gazes when you consider all the people traveling behind you on the highway. So, I decided to pay special attention to the mahogany trim at the rear and the light fixtures and license plate. I assembled the parts from left-over pieces from the trim and cut and shaped them with hand tools.

(1)

1. Make a license plate frame.

A custom license plate frame made from mahogany trim scraps and ¼-inch plywood adds a special custom feel to the design and provides a sturdy mounting plate for the light fixture.

2. Create custom brake lights.

The brake light mounting plates match the design of the license plate frame. Space the plates evenly on either side of the license and mount with screws.

3. Craft the exterior light mounting plates.

Mahogany mounting plates are easy to make. Rough-shape each piece and cut out the center to make room for the wires.

4. Mount the light.

Screw the mahogany mounting plate to the trailer and then attach the fixture to it.

12.4
Aluminum trim

Aluminum trim comes in a variety of extruded shapes and dimensions. However, unless you live near a source, most of your shopping will be done on the Internet. So, finding the right profiles to match the trailer design and its functional needs can be a bit of a guessing game.

I found a friendly seller online called Vintage Technologies whose proprietor, Frank Bear, was happy to guide me through the selection process. Bear is a long-time builder of teardrop trailers and also runs a parts-retailing business to support DIY enthusiasts like me. With his help, I ordered up a few options of trim to try out.

Aluminum trim is easy to cut with a chopsaw, bandsaw, or by hand with a coping saw. The material also bends around curves without fuss and installs easily with a bead of silicone and machine screws.

When joining two pieces of trim at a corner, I used miter joints or overlapped them in a way that made the water have to really work to get through. Admittedly, any joining method you use will not provide a perfect watertight seal alone. That's where flashing and silicone adhesive come in.

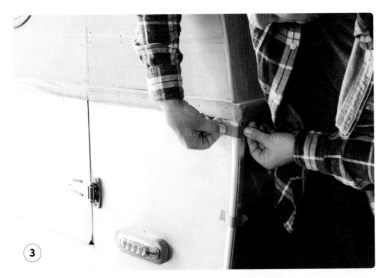

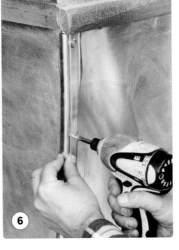

1. Install the fitted edge trim.
For a tight fit, cut a notch into the corner of the tailgate trim to clear the wall on each side. The hatch edge is trimmed with aluminum trim that matches the tailgate. Install rubber seal in between to keep it watertight.

2. Match the trim on the hatch.
Add the aluminum siding to the hatch bottom. The hatch closes on the window trim and overlaps with a matching trim and rubber seal, creating a water barrier.

3. Cut the wide corner trim.
Cut the corner trim to rough size at the front and back. Final fitting will take place during installation.

4. Seal with silicone adhesive.
Apply a thick bead of silicone to the aluminum trim before installing.

5. Pilot drill before installation.
Position the aluminum trim and pilot drill through it and the trailer side to make the final install easy and ensure it's properly aligned when it counts.

6. Attach the trim.
Finally, attach the trim with screws, placed evenly apart. The extra silicone squeeze-out is easy to clean up with a rag.

12.5
Hurricane Hinge

This section is as fun to say as it is to install. The Hurricane Hinge is a legend in the world of teardrop trailers. Its rugged, weatherproof design is built to stand up to wear-and-tear no matter how many times you open and close the rear hatch, and it installs with ease.

To install the Hurricane Hinge, I fit the hatch in place flush and aligned to the trailer body, then drive a row of heavy-duty screws through the hinge to lock it in place. Back in the framing chapter, I intentionally positioned 2 x 2 redwood framing right underneath the hinge to give it some good meat for the screws to grip.

I also installed a mahogany trim piece underneath the hinge. This piece serves a few purposes. It raises the hinge so it's flush with the door surface. It provides additional material for the screws to grab, and it's shaped in a way that redirects water away from the hatch and off the side of the trailer.

1. Install hinge trim.
A pair of matching mahogany trim pieces provide a strong mount for the Hurricane Hinge. The front piece is shaped to redirect water away from the hatch.

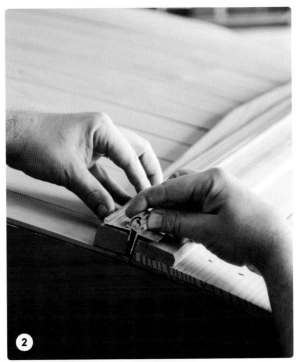

2. Dry-fit the hinge.
Set the hatch door in place with its mahogany trim already glued in place. Then use the hinge to locate the exact position of the trim for the other side.

3. Pilot drill the hinge.
Mark the hole locations on the Hurricane Hinge and pilot drill for each screw. Then place it on the mahogany trim piece and drill a pilot hole.

4. Secure the hinge.
Triple check to make sure everything is lined up, then start driving the screws. I secured each end first, then worked my way evenly toward the center.

12.6
Gas-shock props

Gas-shock props easily lift and hold the rear hatch open, just like the ones you see holding open the back window of a camper shell on a pickup truck. However, it is important to select correctly rated props to make sure your hatch closes easily, and doing the math to figure out where to place them can be painstaking.

For example, a pair of props rated at 120 pounds each means together they can hold a hatch up to 240 pounds. If your hatch is like mine, it weighs just a fraction of that. If you install props that are too strong, when you try to close the hatch, it won't budge. You'd have to hang on the hatch to compress the gas-shocks enough to close them.

The second consideration is the math required for placing them. For these reasons, gas-shock props are not always the best choice for first-time builders. Frank Bear of Vintage Technologies said he doesn't usually recommend them. "The geometry is what kills me. The door weighs differently at different points."

Frank has perfected the geometry for his classic teardrop design, which is available as a DIY kit, but placing the props correctly on custom designs requires some math.

I'm not great at math either, so I relied on two key measurements. When opened, the props would need to be fully extended, or just under the 20-inch reach. When closed, the props would be compressed, no less than the 12-inch distance between the two mounting points. There was only one place on my hatch where the prop could be mounted and meet these key requirements, so that's where I put it.

A 60-pound pair worked well for me. I must have done the math right because the door opens slowly with a pillowy landing and closes gently with one hand. Achievement unlocked!

①

1. Watch out for the wrong way.
The gas-shock props install in either direction, but that doesn't mean they work both ways. When installed with the piston on the bottom, the hatch swings open and lands hard.

2. Make sure it's the right way.
Meanwhile, when installed with the piston at the top, the door opens and gently slows to a stop in the full open position.

3. Open and close the hatch.
A pair of 60-pound gas-shock props allows the hatch door to easily and safely open and close.

12.7
Doors and window trim

I'm not gonna lie. Closing up the doors and front window hatch was a real pain in the buttocks. And my confidence level in its long-term ability to keep the water out is not super high. If you decided to use manufactured doors, you can skip this section and move on.

My solution was to cobble together a collection of trim pieces that—when closed—overlap to create a weatherproof seal where the door and the door opening meet. This ensures that water will slough off rather than penetrating the seams between boards.

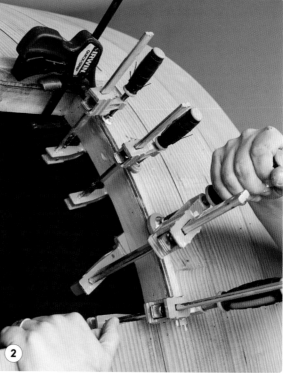

1. Install a hefty hinge mount.
A thick mahogany trim at the top edge of the hatch provides a sturdy mounting base for the second Hurricane Hinge.

2. Add window trim.
Mahogany trim around the front window raises the trim edge so the hatch seals when closed.

3. Mind the gap.
The gap between the door and opening provides room to install a weatherproofing system from mahogany and aluminum trim and rubber weather-stripping.

4. Handmade handle.
I carved a handle for the rear hatch from mahogany scraps.

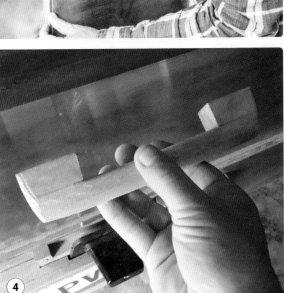

12.8
Trim out the kitchen

By the time I got to this stage in the project, April was halfway through and the summer camping season was calling my name. So, I didn't spend a lot of time tricking out the kitchen with fancy doors, fixtures, or appliances. I figured I'll have plenty of time to remodel the space once I get a better sense of how it will be used.

To keep things simple, I decided to outfit the kitchen space primarily for storage. All of the cooking and prepping will be done on portable equipment set up at the campsite. This keeps the greasy pans and odiferous aromas away from the sleeping quarters, which is especially important in areas with bears or aggressive wildlife.

1. Finish up the power station.
The circuit breaker is mounted into the galley with a simple plywood box that hides the wires and creates a little storage space for a hand-held fire extinguisher.

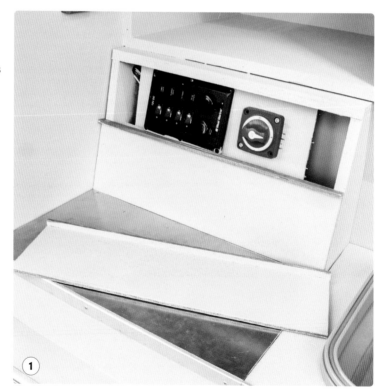

2. Hide the battery box.
Below the power console is a storage box to house the deep-cycle marine battery and a handful of tools to troubleshoot on the road.

3. Mount the ice box.
Line the center box with rigid foam insulation and you've got yourself a simple ice box to store perishable foods and cold drinks. A simpler option is to make a space for a portable cooler.

4. Install the sink basin.
Three-gallon water jugs fit neatly in the upper cabinets. A collapsible basket makes for a simple sink basin below.

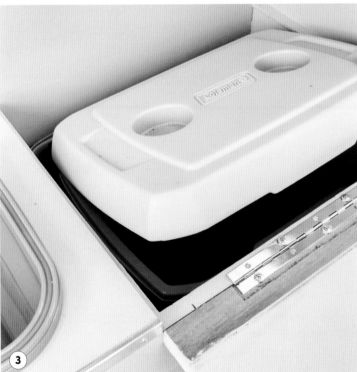

12.9
Roof vent

1. Fit the roof vent.
Install mahogany trim around the perimeter of the roof vent, cut to fit the slight curve of the roof. Adhere the trim to the roof with marine adhesive and clamps.

2. Set the vent.
Set the vent in place with sticky adhesive tape.

3. Make a tight fit.
Screw the vent through the trim and into the trailer framing to tighten up all of the seals and keep things watertight.

TESTING TRIM CONCEPTS

Installing the trim is your last chance to keep the water out. It takes some exploration to come up with the wood trim profiles for the various parts of the trailer build. Here are a few sketches that led me to the final result.

MAHOGANY DETAILS

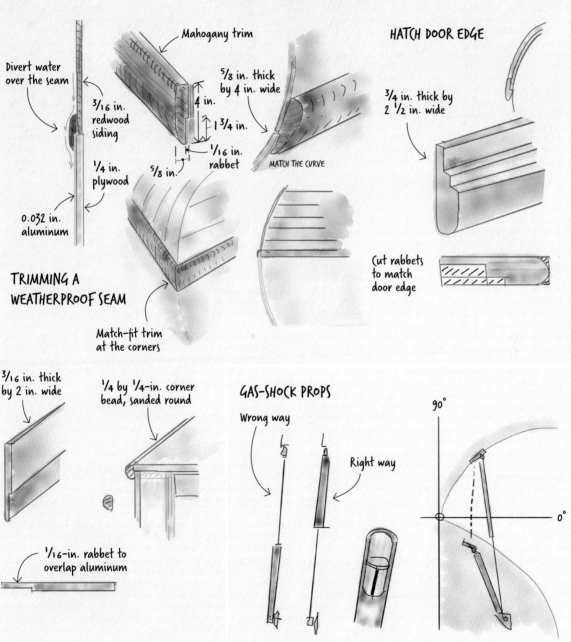

Divert water over the seam

Mahogany trim

5/8 in. thick by 4 in. wide

4 in.

1 3/4 in.

1/16 in. rabbet

5/8 in.

3/16 in. redwood siding

1/4 in. plywood

0.032 in. aluminum

MATCH THE CURVE

HATCH DOOR EDGE

3/4 in. thick by 2 1/2 in. wide

Cut rabbets to match door edge

TRIMMING A WEATHERPROOF SEAM

Match-fit trim at the corners

3/16 in. thick by 2 in. wide

1/4 by 1/4-in. corner bead, sanded round

1/16-in. rabbet to overlap aluminum

GAS-SHOCK PROPS

Wrong way

Right way

90°

0°

— *Apply a* —
WEATHERPROOF FINISH

This final step in the build is where all those efforts to protect the trailer from water, weather, and road debris come together. Depending on the materials of your build, your level of effort will vary. An all-aluminum trailer is low effort: just some basic surface prep and a clear-coat finish to keep it from oxidizing when exposed to nature.

My decision to use redwood as an exterior material increased the level of effort by a huge factor. A wood finish would need to not only protect the wood from weather, but actually seal and fill small cracks and blemishes to keep water from intruding, as well as being able to deal with wood movement.

I decided on an epoxy resin base coat with an outdoor polyurethane topcoat for additional UV protection. This is a durable finish, but will require continual maintenance over time.

13.1

Finishing advice from a pro

There are a handful of tutorial videos on the Internet that demonstrate the application process for epoxy resin. I'm more of a hands-on learner and tracked down a local wooden surfboard maker for an in-person lesson. Martijn Stiphout crafts elaborate wooden surfboards out of his one-man shop in Santa Cruz, California. His process relies on epoxy resin as an adhesive during assembly and as a final finish, and his results are amazing.

He suggested I seal the trailer and fill the cracks with epoxy, and then wipe on a polyurethane finish on top for additional buildup and UV protection.

At Martijn's advice, I purchased 1½ gallons of Super Sap CLR epoxy resin: 2 parts CLR Epoxy, 1 part CLF hardener. I also got a can of West System filleting blend to use as a thickening agent on the filler coat. Martijn demonstrated his technique for me on a small sample section of redwood. Here's his approach:

The first batch of epoxy gets thickened with an additive and goes on with a squeegee. This filler coat fills all the cracks and holes where water might get through. When the epoxy dries, give it a modest sand with 180-grit sandpaper to flatten the surface for the next coat.

The next application is called the cheater coat and is meant to condition the entire surface of wood in preparation for the finish coat. Freshly sanded redwood is thirsty and will suck up a lot of the epoxy when applied. The cheater coat takes care of that and allows the next coat to go on like glass. Use a squeegee to apply this coat of epoxy and then pass over the trailer with a paintbrush. A final glass coat completes the process. Thanks to gravity, drip marks are inevitable on the side walls. Light sanding with 220-grit sandpaper removes those.

Now you have a flat, glassy, sealed surface that's nearly good enough to hit the road. However, epoxy doesn't hold up well to ultraviolet light, and will cloud or crack if it spends a lot of time under the sun. Wipe on a few coats of exterior polyurethane for added UV protection. I found a few exterior finish products from my local hardware store. Go with your favorite.

1. Prep the surface.
Prepare the wood surface with sandpaper for a smooth and blemish-free surface.

2. Thicken the first batch.
Mix the epoxy with a thickening additive to use for filling the cracks and holes. Be careful with this stuff. Wear a respirator and keep the dust well contained. It's toxic!

3. Apply the filler coat.
Apply the thickened epoxy to the seams and nail holes with a squeegee. Push the material across the surface until it's evenly applied.

4. Apply the cheater coat.
Apply a non-thickened layer of epoxy over the filler coat and watch the redwood drink up the material like a desert flower on the first rainy day. Finish up with the final glass coat and exterior polyurethane.

13.2

The right workshop conditions

When I got back to my garage shop I felt confident about the process but was still unsure about how my trailer would turn out. What I did know was that good preparation and planning makes the difference.

Start with a workspace that is dust free and temperature controlled to ensure the epoxy mixes and sets up properly and dries without dust and debris. Also, stock up on plenty of supplies and safety gear. You'll need a scale for measuring the 2-part blend, a few mixing buckets, squeegee tools, paintbrushes, rubber gloves, mixing sticks, sandpaper, and rags or shop towels for cleanup. Lay them out for easy access in an emergency.

Be safe. Keep the epoxy off your skin, clothes, and the garage floor. And keep the dust well contained when sanding (or go outside). Most of all, take your time. Let each coat dry according to the manufacturer's recommendation. Sand well between coats, especially if the epoxy dries with noticeable drips or brush marks.

①

1. Mask the trailer.
Cover all the aluminum surfaces and the area around the trailer to prevent epoxy drips.

2. Seal the cracks with filler coat.
Mix filler into the first batch of epoxy to thicken the material for filling the cracks and holes. Apply it with a squeegee to fill all the cracks, seams, and nail holes.

3. Squeegee on the cheater coat.
Mix up small batches of epoxy and work your way around the entire trailer, applying epoxy evenly to the entire surface. Brush away drips.

4. Look out for drips.
The epoxy will inevitably sag as it dries on the side walls, leaving noticeable drip marks.

5. Sand between coats.
Buff out the surface after each application with 320-grit sandpaper to smooth out the bumps and drips for the next application.

1

2

3

4

6. Brush on the glass coat.
The next coat of epoxy really makes the wood grain pop, especially if you've done a good job sanding and prepping for each application.

7. Add UV protection.
Add a top coat of exterior polyurethane finish to give the finish additional UV protection and build up the finish.

8. Buff in the finish.
Wrap a cotton cloth around a balled-up rag and soak it in finish. Then polish the trailer to a glossy finish, moving the applicator in small circular motion.

9. Bring out the figure.
After the finish has dried, you can see how much the figure and grain patterns are set off by the epoxy.

10. Conduct the waterproof test.
After the finish is applied, give it a test run with the garden hose to make sure there's nowhere for the water drips to intrude.

6

7

13.3
Aluminum clear coat

It's tough keeping the surface of the aluminum siding on the trailer in pristine shape. By the time I finished building, the aluminum looked like it had already traveled 1,000 miles.

A good way of dealing with this inevitable marring is to embrace the scratches. You can "brush" the surface and finish it with a clear-coat. Make sure there is no moisture trapped beneath your clearcoat. That will cause aluminum corrosion and blemish the surface over time.

Use safety precautions when sanding aluminum. Work in a well-ventilated area. Wear a respirator and gloves and keep the fine dust out of your living and working quarters.

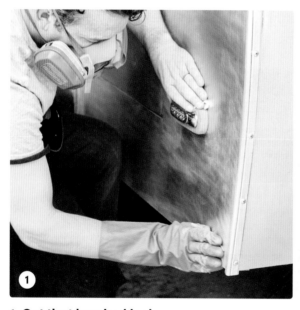

1. Get that brushed look.
Hand-sand the surface with 320-grit wet-dry sand paper. Make passes across the aluminum surface with straight even strokes.

2. Wipe on protection.
Wipe on or spray on a clear-coat finish on top of the aluminum to protect it from oxidation.

13.4
Interior woodwork

I kept things fast and simple for the interior woodwork to offer basic protection from dirt, moisture, and camping wear-and-tear. I went with a pint of exterior paint from the hardware store. Paint helps to hide the inevitable dings and scratches on the plywood and gave the trailer a nice pop of color.

An alternative approach to keep the plywood grain visible is to brush on a few coats of water-based polycrylic. It goes on quickly without much fuss and is easy to clean up. Over the course of the trailer's life, the interior will require some touch-up, so I decided not to be too precious about the finish.

I also decided to leave the cabin interior unfinished for now. Cedar is weather-resistant and I don't want the interior to smell like wood finish.

1. Add a splash of color.
A fresh coat of exterior paint pulls the kitchen interior together and makes the galley pop with color.

(14)

LET'S GO CAMPING!

This chapter begins on the side of the road, in a small California agriculture town, across the street from a fast-food restaurant and autobody shop where my wife, two kids, and I were eating homemade sandwiches and cold veggies and dip from the back of the teardrop trailer. Salinas, California, is not a picturesque kind of place, even though it was made famous by John Steinbeck, but its fertile ground is responsible for growing nearly half of the nation's lettuce, strawberries, and veggies. Its central location on the road from the Monterey Bay to Highway 101 also makes it a perfect spot to pull over for a pit stop. It was here on our first family camping trip with trailer in tow that I realized all that work and effort was worth it. Fixing your own impromptu meals in a fully stocked kitchen on a family road trip is just one of the many benefits of owning a teardrop trailer.

Plenty of storage means you can easily carry a lot of campsite gear. Our family of four takes turns spending the night in the trailer or the tent.

I spent the day before our first trip preparing and packing, and indulged in a shopping spree at the nearby Container Store, where I picked up a variety of bins to hold food, utilities, electronics, and other belongings. I brought a tape measure and my kitchen galley measurements, aiming for a collection of shapes and sizes that went together with a Tetris-like fit. I stocked the kitchen with food, cooking supplies, pots and pans, the cooler, and a bunch of tools and materials that might come in handy. I definitely overpacked, but that's okay because there was room and weight capacity.

FIRST TIME OUT

Our first trip took us among the coastal oaks, twisted manzanita, and towering redwoods, just a short 30-minute drive over the Santa Cruz Mountains at Henry Cowell Redwoods State Park.

We pulled up to the ranger station to check into our campsite and found ourselves in line behind another teardrop trailer. Good omen. We high-fived, inspected each other's rigs, and headed off to our respective campsites.

Next came my first experience backing up. I was circling the campsite for our spot and made a wrong turn, getting myself into a pickle on a one-way road. I only managed to get out of it by the lucky placement of some big trees and boulders. The second time backing up got us parked at our site. It was a textbook success, but I wasn't exactly sure how I did it.

After unloading camp chairs and setting up the tent, we were settled in. Prepping dinner was easy thanks to the prepping surfaces and easy-to-access storage. After dinner, we loaded up the removable sink basin with the dirty dishes and washed them at the nearby spigot.

As sunset neared, my kids started to pester us about sleeping in the trailer. I held my ground; Mom and Dad got dibs on the teardrop for the inaugural night. The kids agreed to the tent but after some expert negotiating they brokered a deal to take turns—one night parents, one night kids, with mixing and matching allowed if all parties agreed.

Later that night when everyone was sufficiently s'mored and tired, we retreated to our sleeping quarters. Just as we were dozing off in bed, comfy and warm in the cool coastal night, I thought out loud to my wife: "What if someone drove a truck up to the trailer, hitched us up, and drove off with us inside?!" We had a good laugh at the thought. The following week I bought a lock for the ball hitch to secure it from thieves when it's disconnected.

DESINATION: HARMONY

Our reservation at Henry Cowell was up, but we weren't ready to go home. So we continued driving south to the California Central Coast for a night in Harmony,

When camping in the Sierras, no food is allowed in the galley kitchen to prevent bears from coming around.

California, population 18. Two of those are my in-laws, and they let us park out front with a sprawling view of the golden hillsides. Harmony is not just the name of the town, it also describes the feeling it invokes when all you can hear is the wind and coyotes lull you to sleep.

We awoke to our first light rain; a welcome test of water resistance. All looked well, but it reminded me I still needed to run a waterproof test. When I got home, I drenched the trailer from every angle with a garden hose. Lo and behold, a stream of water started pouring into the cabin just above the front window hatch. Most of the water was backing up on the trim and redirecting around the window to each side as designed. But a tiny gap between the trailer siding and trim was letting water through, right onto the driver's side pillow. It was an easy fix. I mixed up a cup of epoxy resin and poured it over the leaky joint. Voila, leak sealed.

MOUNTAIN LIFE

Our second trip took us 8,000 feet up to the Sierra Nevada mountain range, near South Lake Tahoe beneath the towering ponderosa pines. Up here in bear country, the park rangers require all visitors to store their food, drinks, and scented liquids in a bombproof bear box provided at each campsite. So we packed the trailer accordingly: no food or smelly things that might attract the bears. The kitchen galley was re-purposed as a utility workspace and activity cabinet, with games, sports equipment, tools, and flashlights; a convenient place to store hats and keys and charge phones and camera at the campsite.

When traveling the interior is packed with gear and all the campsite belongings, making sure to distribute the weight properly. When parked at the campsite, the inside turns into a comfy queen-sized bedroom.

A pop tent provides shade from the hot, damaging Silicon Valley sun, while the fitted cover protects the trailer from the elements. Now if only there was a way to keep the spiders out.

The air up there was thin and dry, and the sun was hot: great conditions to test the resilience of the redwood siding. Remember, wood shrinks and expands with changes in humidity, and these conditions were definitely testing the science. Over the course of two days, I could literally see the 8-inch-wide redwood panels contracting. A sliver of a gap opened between two boards in a few isolated spots. When we got home I left the trailer in the driveway exposed to the intense Silicon Valley heat for two days and the small cracks turned big. Uh oh. Now water could get in. I didn't panic; I patched the area with thickened epoxy

and applied two more coats of finish over the entire top surface. Then I invested in a high-quality fitted cover and a pop-up tent to provide shade from the direct sun.

We have more family trips planned this summer before school starts to test out the trailer in a variety of camping and weather conditions. I fully expect that each trip will bring new lessons learned and provide new opportunities for maintenance, upgrades, and repair. Already my aluminum finish is wearing thin. And the kitchen paint job could use some touch-ups. Good news is, I know who to call when something needs fixing.

15

The Teardrop Trailer
OWNER'S MANUAL

Congratulations to you: the new owner of a handmade teardrop trailer! After so many hours in the garage invested in craftsmanship, waterproofing, and road safety, it's finally time to put it all to the test on the road. If you are a first-time trailer owner like me, this final chapter introduces you to the basic rules of the road to help ensure you operate your trailer safely and enjoy it for many years to come.

LICENSE AND REGISTRATION, PLEASE

In North America, trailers and RVs are subject to a set of federal regulations and industry standards designed to keep dangerous vehicles off the roads. Regulations like the location and number of vehicle lights are spelled out in the trailer-related sections of the Federal Motor Vehicle Safety Standards and guidelines set by the Society of Automotive Engineers, or SAE. Each state has its own interpretation of these rules and regulations that must be met to register your trailer and get a license plate.

Good news: If you purchased a utility trailer from a dealer like I did, it should come with a Vehicle Identification Number (VIN) filed with the Department of Transportation and a state license plate.

After adding all my additional luxuries on top of the utility trailer, I wanted to make sure I was still road legal. So, I scheduled an appointment at the nearby California DMV and rolled up to the parking lot on a sunny weekday afternoon. There's no option on the DMV website or

phone tree for "upgraded my utility trailer to a handmade teardrop trailer" so I didn't really know what to expect. I figured they would either wave me away uninterested or pull out a clipboard and tape measure and give it a thorough inspection.

WELCOME TO THE DMV

I arrived 15 minutes early at the DMV for my 2 pm appointment and took my place in a long line for reservation holders. I was reciting in my head how to explain my situation and was prepared to stump them. As if she'd seen everything before, the woman at the reception desk listened to my situation and began rooting around her files and computer to confirm her suspicions.

She explained that I only needed to change the body type on the title to reflect that it was modified from "Utility Trailer" to "Camp Trailer." She handed me a document to fill out and directed me to the waiting area for my number to be called.

The woman at the next window also seemed upbeat. She inspected my original title from the dealer and confirmed my VIN and registration in the system. She explained that my situation required an in-person inspection to verify that the lights were up to spec, that the trailer was not intended for permanent residence, and that it did not exceed length and width requirements. In California, trailers longer than 16 feet are designated as "Coach" and pay an annual registration fee like a car, versus every five years like a utility trailer. Also, she said, no weigh-in required since only commercial trailers pay fees for weight.

As she keyed away on her green screen, I quizzed the clerk on a few other curiosities. "What if I had built my trailer completely from scratch and didn't have a VIN?" I asked. She explained that the DMV would assign one for me during the inspection using a standard coding pattern.

She provided me with a paper form and told me to drive the trailer around to the vehicle verification area where an agent would be waiting to help, then return with my completed documents.

A friendly man with a clipboard met me there. He was familiar with this inspection process; after more than a decade on duty he told me he's encountered a few handmade trailers like mine (though none as nice looking). But it was a rare event, so he went inside to grab a newer colleague and use this as a training opportunity.

Admiring my handiwork, the man began checking off the boxes and filling out his form. One axle, check. Two wheels, check. Not a permanent dwelling, check. Functioning travel lights, brake lights, and blinkers, check. Less than 16 feet long, check. Less than 85 inches wide, check. He sent me back inside with completed paperwork and a pleasant handshake.

That's when things started to fall apart. The vehicle inspector checked all the right boxes, but when the woman entered them into the computer, the system would not accept them. She called over her manager, who was equally as stumped. Eventually, the manager walked away, leaving my clerk with no choice but to enter my trailer in as a "Coach." For a year of registration and fees past due, I owed $580 please.

Things did not feel right. I believed the inspector who categorized it as a "Camp Trailer" over the antiquated computer system. So, I halted the transaction and told the clerk I'd be back after I did some more research. She agreed and suggested visiting a different DMV to find someone with more experience on the subject.

Until then, I'll keep the title as a "Utility Trailer," which is adequate for now.

If your goals are bigger than just making one trailer for yourself—perhaps you believe there's a market for selling trailers to family and friends—make sure you do your research. Trailer manufacturers are required of meet a strict set of requirements and regulations. A good place to start if you're interested in going pro is the National Association of Trailer Manufacturers, or NATM, which runs a compliance verification program for makers.

SELECTING THE RIGHT VEHICLE

Much of the appeal of a teardrop trailer is its tiny, compact size. But be careful how small you go with the vehicle that pulls it. Manufacturers usually provide maximum tow ratings, but that number can be deceiving. Your capacity must also account for the weight of each passenger, and your luggage and load.

To illustrate, let's use my trusty 2007 Honda Odyssey: It has a manufacturer's recommended tow capacity of 2,700 pounds. Loaded up for a trip to the woods, it contains 450 pounds of humans (two adults and two kids), 150 pounds of clothes and camping gear, and 100 pounds of food and water. That brings the max towing capacity to 2,000 pounds. My trailer weighs in at about 1,400 pounds dry, which leaves 600 pounds of additional carrying capacity. I'm happy with that.

If you push your car past its recommended limit, you start putting extra stress on the transmission, brakes, and chassis. It may even void your warranty. Vehicles that are built for pulling trailers will typically beef up these components and add a tow package that comes with a hardwired brake controller and 7-pin hitch plug.

HITCHING AND UNHITCHING

When I picked up my trailer from the dealer, it didn't leave the lot until the hitch connection passed a 10-point inspection. I kept that checklist in my glove box and refer to it every time I take the trailer out on the road. It's a good habit.

1. Receiver hitch, ball mount, pin, and clip engaged
2. Trailer coupler latched and locked
3. Safety chains crossed
4. Safety latches engaged on safety chains
5. Tongue jack and wheel in the full upright position
6. Brake lights, travel lights, and blinkers working
7. Break-away brake cable connected
8. Electrical brakes functioning, and brake controller adjusted
9. All trailer wheel lug nuts/bolts torqued to 95 pounds
10. All doors and hatches are closed, and objects inside are secured.

It's not a bad idea to be cautious and recheck these throughout your road trip. Safety first and foremost!

DRIVER'S ED: TURNING, BACKING UP, AND PARKING

If you're a newbie, it takes some practice to get the knack of driving your trailer on the open road. When you add 12 feet to the back of your vehicle and attach it at a pivot point, all bets are off.

Before you plan your first big road trip, work your way up with a few small- and medium-sized expeditions around your neighborhood. Take it out around the block a few times. Find yourself a two-lane thoroughfare. Eventually work your way up to highway traveling.

Becoming a good driver with a trailer in tow is as much about mastering the technical maneuvering as it is about mentally preparing yourself for the drive. You'll encounter impatient drivers who expect you to speed ahead or make room for them even when it's not convenient. Take a deep breath and respond only when it's safe to

do so. If the emotional stress of their road rage is too much to handle, avoid eye contact and stay positive until they drive by. Here are some other useful tips from the teardrop trailer community:

1. Travel at a safe speed limit. This isn't a race. You're on vacation. Travel at or under the speed limit for your safety and the safety of everyone else on the road. As for those impatient drivers around you, or tailgating you, ignore them. And pull over to let them pass if they're too aggressive or the line of cars stacks up.
2. Travel in a caravan with other recreational vehicles. There's strength in numbers. Caravanning makes it clear to other drivers they just need to go around.
3. Swing wide on your turns. It's easy to mis-judge and end up clipping a sidewalk, or worse—a telephone pole or parked car.
4. Backing up is hard! Set aside your instincts; everything you've learned about navigating in reverse is about to get turned inside out. To direct a trailer backward, your steering wheel control is backward: turn the wheel counterclockwise to direct the trailer back and to the right. Turn the wheel clockwise to direct it back and to the left.
5. Too sharp of a turn in reverse will cause your trailer to jack-knife, putting you in a tight predicament, which can only be resolved by driving forward to straighten out. It can also cause the front corner of the trailer to crash into your vehicle—scratching the paint at best and leaving a big dent at worst.
6. Avoid conflict. In life I've found you can save yourself a lot of strife if you follow this motto. That's my strategy for parking a trailer while on a road trip. When stopping for food and drink, sight-seeing, or bathroom breaks, I look for malls, grocery stores, and big-box or discount retailers. Then I head to the back of the parking lot.
7. If you do find yourself parking on a side street or neighborhood road, parallel parking should be reserved only for the most talented trailer operators. You need a good run-way

no matter which way you park—in reverse or by pulling in front first.

8. Don't let the chains drag while driving; that can send sparks shooting from the vehicle that can ignite dry vegetation and cause wildfires.

9. Turn off the on-board electricity and unhook gas lines if you have one before driving.

10. Shut all the windows and doors and secure them tightly so they don't swing open or fly off while driving.

11. Check your trailer brakes regularly and familiarize yourself with how to manually operate them in an emergency.

12. Now that you're comfortable on the road, stay vigilant with your packing. Remember that 40/60 rule that came up back in chapter three (page 61) when setting the dimensions of the trailer? Keep that in mind again when packing for a road trip.

13. Keep some airflow into the trailer for balanced air pressure when traveling up and down great variations in altitude. An imbalance in air pressure with the outside environment creates crushing pressure on the trailer. Imagine a half-empty bottle of water on an airplane. When you reach cruising altitude, the bottle will compress to balance the air pressure. The same thing can happen with your trailer. Only, rather than crumpling up or exploding out, the pressure will exploit any small cracks or openings in the trailer shell and pull air in or out under intense vacuum pressure. If there's water outside—say it's raining on the drive up to the top of a mountain—the vacuum pressure can suck water through the tiniest cracks, and travel past bends and turns. A common solution to prevent this extreme cabin-pressure variation is to install small vents to the outside.

SAFETY AT THE CAMPSITE

Once you're parked at the campsite, your trailer will become a refuge of safety and comfort versus the stress of pulling it on the open road. There are a few safety things to keep in mind.

First, make sure the trailer is planted securely, especially if you're parked on an incline. Position wheel stops on both sides of each tire. Raise the front wheel (if you have one) and lower the front hitch post to transfer the trailer tongue weight to it.

Second, sleep with the windows open. Running out of fresh air in a closed-up teardrop trailer is a very real concern. Because of the tiny space inside your trailer you should *always* keep a vent or window open to ensure you have an ample supply of oxygen, no matter the weather.

As one Internet forum member noted: "It's better to be a little cold than a little dead."

OFF-SEASON STORAGE AND MAINTENANCE

When you're not on the road enjoying your trailer, keep it stored in a dry safe place to extend its life. Exposure to water can damage your trailer with mold or mildew. This is difficult to repair and hazardous to your health. So, do everything you can to prevent long-term exposure to rain, morning dew, and heavy condensation.

While sun and warm weather can help dry out a damp trailer, exposing it to direct sunlight can also break down the wood finish, causing it to cloud and eventually crack. At the very least, keep it covered with a quality canvas cover. Parking it underneath a pop-up tent, carport, or inside the garage is encouraged.

Take extra time to seal up all the trailer openings completely before storing it long term. All the vents, windows, and doors should be completed closed to prevent creepy crawly bugs from taking residence in your trailer.

If you follow the advice in this book, you shouldn't have any trouble maintaining your trailer for the long run. After all, you built it. But it's also important to take good notes during your build to keep track of things that ultimately get hidden behind walls and forgotten. Specifically, note the location of all your wires. Ensure easy access to electrical connections and fixtures in case you need to repair or replace them.

The goal of my project, and this book, is to help you create a recreational vehicle that is long lasting and holds up to any challenge and adventure you tow it to. But just like any heirloom project, you should expect to put some time and effort into keeping it well maintained and repaired.

METRIC CONVERSIONS

In this book, I've used inches, yards, ounces, and pounds, showing anything less than one as a fraction. If you want to convert those to metric measurements, please use the following formulas:

Fractions to Decimals

⅛ = .125

¼ = .25

½ = .5

⅝ = .625

¾ = .75

Imperial to Metric Conversion

Length

Multiply inches by 25.4 to get millimeters

Multiply inches by 2.54 to get centimeters

Multiply yards by .9144 to get meters

For example, if you wanted to convert 1 ⅛ inches to millimeters:

1.125 in. x 25.4 mm = 28.575 mm

And to convert 2 ½ yards to meters:

2.5 yd. x .9144 m = 2.286 m

Weight

Multiply ounces by 28.35 to get grams

Multiply pounds by .45 to get kilograms

For example, if you wanted to convert 5 ounces to grams:

5 oz. x 28.35 g = 141.75 g

And to convert 2 pounds to kilograms:

2 lb. x .45 kg = .9 kg

ABOUT THE AUTHOR

Matt Berger, Californian designer and builder of everyday objects, is the author of *The Handmade Skateboard* (Spring House Press, 2014). A lifelong hobby enthusiast and workshop adventurer, Matt makes a living helping companies design and build digital products, and makes a passion out of helping others design and build physical objects in his garage workshop and local maker spaces. Matt earned his stripes in the woodshop as an editor at *Fine Woodworking* magazine, where he launched FineWoodworking. com, and produced and starred in how-to videos for the Web site. Matt applied all the skills learned and practiced at the Fine Woodworking shop to create a series of

workshops teaching students of all ages how to build a handmade skateboard. That turned into his first book and the DIY brand SK8Makers. With his second book, *The Handmade Teardrop Trailer*, Matt is expanding his DIY ambitions to a much bigger project.

ACKNOWLEDGEMENTS

Designing and building a project of this scale—and then turning it into a book—is not a solo project. There are many people I'd like to thank for supporting and contributing to the making of this book. First, my editor, Matthew Teague, for suggesting the idea, which he originally pitched as a mobile woodshop to run traveling SK8Makers workshops. To the amazing team of women who sorted through my giant pile of photos, drawings, captions, and text to assemble this beautifully designed, produced, and edited book: thank you Lindsay Hess, Jodie Delohery, and Kerri Grzybicki (respectively). To the trailer and RV community of experts who shared their knowledge with me and helped guide me through the tough parts: Jack Kantola, a fellow woodworker, former RV executive, mentor, and friend; and the entire team of technicians and sales managers at Orlandi Trailer. To all my friends and neighbors who stopped by my garage over the course of the project to share tips, expertise, tools, and encouragement, especially Paul Hummel, who is in my opinion an "expert-of-all-trades." To my landlord Cosimo and the entire Giancola family for your encouragement and support while I took over your two-car garage with sawdust and tools. And especially to my family, far and wide: Mom, Dad, Step Mom, Big Bros, Big Sis, Wife, and Daughters 1 and 2: thank you all for putting up with my crazy ideas.

INDEX

MORE GREAT BOOKS *from*
SPRING HOUSE PRESS

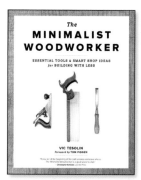

The Minimalist Woodworker
978-1-940611-35-8
$24.95 | 152 Pages

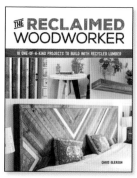

The Reclaimed Woodworker
978-1-940611-54-9
$24.95 | 168 Pages

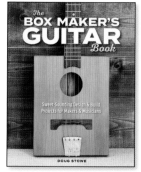

The Box Maker's Guitar Book
978-1-940611-64-8
$24.95 | 168 Pages

CNC Router Essentials
978-1-940611-52-5
$24.95 | 144 Pages

**SketchUp Success
for Woodworkers**
978-1-940611-68-6
$24.95 | 160 Pages

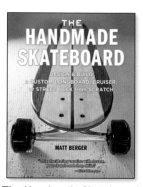

The Handmade Skateboard
978-1-940611-06-8
$24.95 | 160 Pages

Make Your Own Knife Handles
978-1-940611-53-2
$22.95 | 168 Pages

Make Your Own Cutting Boards
978-1-940611-45-7
$22.95 | 168 Pages

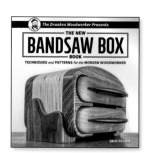

The New Bandsaw Box Book
978-1-940611-32-7
$19.95 | 120 Pages

SPRING HOUSE PRESS

Look for these Spring House Press titles at your favorite bookstore, specialty retailer, or visit *www.springhousepress.com*.
For more information about Spring House Press, call 1-717-569-5196 or email us at *info@springhousepress.com*.